The H
of the New Testament

He is the mediator of a new covenant
(Hebrews 9 : 15)

by
JOHN B. CHAMPION, A.M., Th.D.
PROFESSOR OF CHRISTIAN DOCTRINE
Eastern Baptist Theological Seminary
Philadelphia, Pennsylvania

ZONDERVAN PUBLISHING HOUSE
GRAND RAPIDS MICHIGAN

EIGHT-FIFTEEN FRANKLIN STREET
GRAND RAPIDS, MICHIGAN

To
Joseph T. Beardwood, Jr.
A.B., M.D., F.A.C.P.

FOREWORD

THIS is a study of the greatest of subjects—*The Heart of the New Testament,* which is the redeeming Sacrifice of God in Christ. Our very destiny lies in what we think on this theme. What is the human mind for but to ponder on this in such a way as to produce fit response to it? Then prayer should go with it that God be near us, even within us, as we behold the open wounds which the Lord bears for us as sinners. May the Holy Spirit interpret to us the profound truth of this subject that it may possess us. Then the deeps of Divine Redemption shall call unto the deeps of the human soul and to its equally deep need.

Here one explanation should be offered. Throughout the discussion I have capitalized the pronouns expressing Deity. In many places this prevents misunderstanding as to whom they refer. The American Revised Version of the Scriptures has been followed in the main.

To three persons I wish to acknowledge with gratitude my debt for helpful suggestions. First to Professor William W. Adams, Th.D., co-laborer for the past fifteen years in seminary work; also to a younger colleague, Robert G. Torbet, A.M., B.D.; and to the beloved partner of my life, Edith Webster Champion, Th.B.

J. B. C.

Philadelphia, Pennsylvania

CONTENTS

Chapter One

COMPANION TERMS WITH REDEMPTION

Purpose of the Book as a Whole

The purpose of this book is to set forth "The Heart of the New Testament." The Heart of the Old Testament is "The Old Covenant," even as the Heart of the New Testament is "The New Covenant." These covenants will be compared later on in our discussion. First, however, we should give some attention to the great matter which made both covenants necessary. This is the dark and forbidding subject of *sin.* Iniquity is bound to be an unwelcome topic to the sinner. Unless impelled by the Holy Spirit man is sure to avoid discussion of his guilt before God.

I. Iniquity

Our subject compels first consideration of the depths of depravity in iniquity. The meaning we find in salvation and redemption depends upon the meaning we find in that from which we are saved or redeemed. No sound view of salvation is bound to follow inadequate survey of the seriousness of sin. Hence we need first of all to probe "the exceeding sinfulness of sin." The remedy for any disease is counted valuable in proportion to the known danger of and injury by the affliction treated. Appreciation of Redemption comes from holy hate of that which is infinitely worse than any or all physical diseases. Only as "sin appears sin," does the work of the Great Physician come to full meaning and recognition on our part, and Redemption appears Redemption.

Iniquity is a personal product, a self-realization difficult to define. Not only about God does it derange us, but also about sin itself. The more we sin the less we understand it and the Most High who made us. The Scriptures depict this greatest malady of man as the substance of the blackness of spiritual darkness in this world where but for it all would have been light and transparence. As the intrusion of lawlessness in a world of law it is at the same time godlessness in a world of God, selfishness and inhumanity in the world of man. All law in the moral and personal realm is founded on the unfailing regularity of the way God's perfect nature works. He made man to conform to this law. Sin is opposition therefore, not only to Divine law, but to God Himself. Paul and John define iniquity as *anomos*, lawlessness, anarchy (I Tim. 1:19; I John 3:4).

This antagonism to the Most High is dead against the highest human possibility of attainment in and by God, and results in the lowest possibility of realization in degradation. But for iniquity in created personality there could be none anywhere. All else in creation is subject to Divine law and purpose. Capacity for God and freedom of self-determination are constituent in personality. Sinful self-determination is perversion or abuse of this freedom.

Some say, "I do not want to hear about sin." This is vainly attempting to ignore our guilt. Responsibility for our sin will not let us go. "Forget it," say others. This also is equally impossible, for sin's muddle and mischief dogs our days. No one ever knows all he does in committing sin, for it would take a full eternity to realize all it means.

There are three main directions taken by sin: toward God, within human personality, and in relation to fellow-man. These are not mutually exclusive lines of movement. They are rather convenient classifications for the sake of discussion. Sin is anti-God wherever we find it, and anti-man and against the sinner himself. Hence we are bidden, "Seek first the kingdom of God." Redemption is foundationally unto right relation to God and self and fellow-man. It is useless to deny it. The so-called science-religion which puts central in it this negation, "There is no sin," asserts more that Christianity denies, and denies more that Christianity asserts, than any other heresy.

Principal A. M. Fairbairn has said: "Sin is in its positive character the substitution of self for God as the law and end of our being; in its negative character it is transgression of law. . . . There is therefore, to speak with the older theologians, something infinite in sin." [1]

[1] The Place of Christ in Modern Theology, p. 453.

Everything God makes, He puts meaning therein; but sin is the one thing which God did not create; so it remains "the mystery of iniquity." It is "missing the mark" God designed as the end in personal existence. Its power of perversion prevents shooting straight at the target of life eternal, and equally hinders living straight. Iniquity is that morally twisted out of shape, that wrong or wrung out of alignment, the unchanging foe of correspondence with God.

The effect of sin within human personality may be summed up as "selfishness." The futility of this in relation to God or to fellow-man is plain. Then self-stagnation and self-stultification must result from creating this vacuum and trying to live in it. It has filled the world's history with every conceivable form and substance of inhumanity. "Man's inhumanity to man makes countless millions dead" — in these days. Refusing to be his brother's keeper, man misses fulfilment in God; and with that gone, what worth while remains?[2]

II. Redemption

Perhaps the seriousness of sin may best be discerned in considering the remedy for it. Let us therefore look at the meaning of the term *Redemption*. Later and in more extended fashion the full substance of *The New Covenant* will be examined. The terms "Redeemer" and "Redemption" occur frequently in both the Old and the New Testaments (or Covenants). A familiar

[2] The objection that sin is personified may be met with the fact that we do not personify the personal but the impersonal. We cannot personify man. He is a person already. We personalize sin, not personify it. Sin is personal or it is nothing.

passage is Job 19:25, "I know that my Redeemer (*Goel*) liveth." Its cognate verb *gaal* means to purchase, ransom, redeem (usually in the interest of a relative). The word Redeemer (*Lutrōtēs*) occurs in Acts 7:35, but there is translated "deliverer," except in the R. V. margin. The word Redemption with its cognate verb *lutroō* is used many times either with or without *apo*. When with it the meaning is—full redemption, out and out deliverance, ransom. The underlying suggestion in any use of the term is that an obligation, debt or bondage exists. Bondage to Satan was an idea very prominent in the early ages of Christianity, and we find it therefore embodied in the first formal theory of Christ's Redemption. This agreed with the interpreting content of mind at that time. To the Evil One He *became* by and in His death the price of ransom. The deliverance of sinners followed, because Satan could not hold Christ Himself, and thus got cheated out of both possession and price.

1. It is true that sin does put sinners in the hands of Satan to some degree, but this is an utterly illegal and unrighteous possession, for all true possession is in God. The soul being dead to God, personal evil is bound to control it, for in the spiritual world as in this, "nature abhors a vacuum." Something comes in to fill it. Evidently Jesus taught His disciples to pray (Matt. 6:13), "Deliver us from the Evil One." (R.V.) "The evil" in this case could hardly be abstract and impersonal and able to hold in bondage, but must be rather the Evil One with whom Christ Himself con-

tended in the temptation in the wilderness. So also in our Redemption by Christ we are delivered not merely from either abstract evil or evil in ourselves, but from the concrete personal power and empire of ungodly spirits. Schleiermacher calls the confederacy of ungodly spirits "the Kingdom of Sin." Being the father of Modernism, he is still good authority to quote today. At any rate he passed the expression on to the conservative Theodore Haering, who says:

"Individual sinful wills are merged into a kingdom of sin."[3] "Not as a sum of self-centered units, but, in conformity with the general laws of our spiritual being, as a communion of wills reacting upon each other."[4] Haering stands strongly for accepting the Scriptures' account of Satan and evil spirits.

2. An important virtue of the term "Redemption" is its recognition of bondage to a malign power external to ourselves as well as within. The Epistle to the Hebrews says: "Since the children are sharers in blood and flesh (the Greek text order), He also Himself in like manner partook of the same (by the Incarnation); that through death He might bring to naught him that had the power of death, that is, the devil; and might deliver all them who through fear of death were all their lifetime subject to bondage" (Heb. 2: 14, 15).

The real power of Redemption is Christ Himself, but this means is variously stated. In Eph. 1:7, "In whom we have our redemption through His blood." Col. 1:14, "In whom we have our redemption, the forgiveness of

[3] **The Christian Faith** (Eng. Tr.), Vol. I, p. 451.
[4] **The Christian Faith** (Eng. Tr.), Vol I, p. 441.

our sins." Rom. 3:24, "The redemption that is in Christ Jesus." Rev. 5:9, "For Thou wast slain, and didst purchase unto God with Thy blood men of every tribe, and tongue and people and nation; and madest them to be unto our God a kingdom and priests." Here the verb *agorazō*, to redeem by purchase, is used. We may also note here how well the personal point of view is used and maintained in both agent and object in setting forth the process and the means thereof in Redemption as stated in the New Testament.

III. Mediation

In the larger sense the Son of God is Mediator in all the Divine relations with creation. This is true from the work of creation on, where the Father is the Source, the Son the Agent, and the Holy Spirit the life-imparting Person. In relation to sin and sinners Christ is the Sacrificial One who seeks the lost and expresses the Father's love. For those who have obtained through Him right relation to God, He is the Mediator of *a better covenant*, the former one being given through Moses. This Mediation is discussed later in Chapter Five.

1. The Greek term for Mediator is *Mesitēs*. This is from *mesos*, middle. It means a go-between, by implication a reconciler (intercessor). The Mediatorial office of Christ is necessarily grounded in the nature of His Person; and the nature of His Person is indicated by the competent range of His Divine-human powers. Because He has both Divine and Human nature He is

fully qualified to act as Mediator in the covenant of Redemption. There is such vast fulness in His personal nature, powers, offices and sacrifice on our behalf, our terms seem to meet and overlap each other, and prove weak and partial in describing them. Nowhere does this more apply than in the Epistle to the Hebrews. In this He is High Priest and the Offering. He is the New Covenant in two senses, namely, the compact and (as clearly established in the *Koine*) the will and its bequeathment. We find the same richness of fulness in His offices: He is the *Logos*, the Word, God's means of personal expression in all this universe. In the Divine outreach to man He is the Way to God, the Truth about Him we need to know, and the Life in Him, given by Him, and mediated to us as sinners redeemed by His great Sacrifice of Himself. As to this I Tim. 2:5 says, "For there is one God, one Mediator also between God and man, Himself man, Christ Jesus, who gave Himself a ransom for all."

2. We may note here an objection to some of the scripture terms of His Mediation—price, purchase, ransom, and others. These figures of speech are all right if not overworked, misused, or made to "go on all fours," as some of the parables are used. Few metaphors can be taken in quite unrestricted sense. For example, "Application is the cost of education." To whom is the cost paid? To no one! "Eternal vigilance is the price of liberty." To whom is the price paid? Again, to no one! These terms are used subjectively, not objectively. So are the metaphors "ransom" and

"purchase" in the passages quoted. God would not pay Himself, as is objected to concerning the Commercial Theory, namely, that it is like money being taken from one's pocket on one side and put into another pocket on the other side. This could as well apply also to Anselm's eleventh century idea of God honoring His own majesty in the death of Christ. Any metaphor should be truly married to its own definite meaning, and not turned loose in wild polygamy. Spiritualized meanings are taken from passages in a way God never intended. At a prayer and testimony meeting having the topic of "The Triumphal Entry into Jerusalem," an untutored but imaginative brother said: "Everything in Scriptur' is a pictur'. That ass tied where two ways met, is a pictur' of the sinner. To begin with, every sinner is an ass; and he is tied where two ways meet, the way to heaven and the way to hell."

IV. Propitiation

Three Greek terms are used in the five instances in which *propitiation* is mentioned in the New Testament: Heb. 2: 17, *hilaskōmai,* or *hilaskesthai,* a reflexive form meaning to become personally a propitiation—"to make Himself (or, to be made) propitiation," "to expiate the sins of the people." *Hilastērion* (a mercy-seat), *the place of propitiation,* or simply, *propitiation;* Rom. 3: 24, 25, "Being justified freely by His grace through the redemption that is in Christ Jesus: whom God sent forth to be a propitiation, *through faith,* in His blood." In I John 2:2 and 4:10, *hilasmos,* propitiation, "And He is the propitiation for our sins."

"And (God) sent His Son to be the propitiation for our sins." In Paul's addition, *dia pisteos,* we have the important condition, "through faith." This means that Christ's propitiation becomes effective with God in the same way and at the same time that salvation does—by faith. Lastly, in Luke 18:13, *hilaskōmai,* aorist imperative, *hilasthēti,* "God be propitiated (merciful) to me the sinner."

1. The question arises, Why does God need to be propitiated at all? Because of His righteous anger, His holy vexation can be appeased or ended only by the abolition or extermination of iniquity. There is no possible sacrifice for sin that could in the least degree make it agreeable to Him. Unless it could eradicate or blot sin out of existence, the sacrifice of Christ could not allay God's otherwise incurable wrath with iniquity. Hence there was no sufficient palliative effect in even the sacrifice of Christ Himself, if merely to cool God's fierce indignation. He must annihilate sin, nothing less, to redeem fully.

An esteemed liberal professor said to his class in theology: "The God Who propitiates Himself, needs no propitiation." A student replied, "Then the man who feeds himself, needs no food! And the man who washes himself, never needed a bath! And the God Who satisfies Himself, never needed satisfaction!" By his very red face the professor looked as though he did not need embarrassment.

2. Sin's perpetual attitude to God is to blot Him out of existence, so far as the individual sinner is con-

cerned. There can be no mistake about its unrelenting enmity to God despite His absolute righteousness, holiness, and love. In fact there is nothing in God, or that He does, which does not make the sinner hate Him the more. With such irreconcilable enmity there is nothing which can be done in making terms *with it,* for there is not an atom of good to any degree in sin to which God can appeal. If there were, it would not be iniquity. *Now the only thing strong enough in nature to exterminate sin is the direct contact or application of the Divine nature in the Christ's sacrificial Person, Spirit, and redeeming life.* This is because sin comes into existence by no help of God and contrary to His will by anti-divine personal becoming in an immortal nature originally called into being in the likeness of God. Hence this is implied in, "The blood of Jesus His Son cleanseth us from all sin . . . If we confess our sins, He is faithful and just to forgive us our sins, and to cleanse us from all unrighteousness." *This is strategic because effectual.* Unless we take this soundly serious view of iniquity, we can never come to a true view of God's nature in relation to it, and to an adequate estimate of redemption by its obliteration.

V. Reconciliation

God is propitiated, but man is reconciled. The sinner is ever estranged from his God, not God from him. This reconciling may be to God or to a brother who is alienated. Matt. 5:24 says, "First be reconciled to thy brother, and then come and offer thy gift." The Greek word used is *dialassō,* to conciliate. The common word used is *katallassō,* to reconcile. II Cor. 5:19, "God was in Christ reconciling the world unto Himself, not reckoning unto them their trespasses, and having committed unto us the word of reconciliation," *katallagē.* In verses 18, 19 and 20, different forms of this word are used five times; but as above said, the persons are reconciled to God, not God to them—"Who hath reconciled us to Himself through Christ." "Be ye reconciled to God." A stronger form of the word is *apokatallassō,* to reconcile fully, as in Col. 1: 21, "And you being in time past alienated and enemies in your mind in your evil works (22) yet now hath He reconciled in the body of His flesh through death."

1. All the effort and sacrifice toward reconciliation is on the part of God. Hence it would not have been proper to represent God being reconciled to the sinner. God did not need to change. He had not ceased to love and seek after lost mankind. The old hymn, "My God is reconciled," is decidedly wrong and unscriptural in its statement. Nowhere does the Word of God so misrepresent Him. "God in Christ" and "through Christ" express the means of reconciliation. "God so loved the world that He gave His only begotten Son."

VI. Salvation

God is the God of salvation, and the Bible is the Book making it known. We are saved by the Christ of the Bible. The word "salvation" occurs about one hundred and twenty-five times in the Old Testament, and about fifty in the New. In a way salvation is the great theme of the Scriptures as a whole, but in the New Testament "salvation in Jesus Christ" is really its one great theme.

1. The Greek *Sōtēr* means the Saviour; *sōtēria* is salvation; *sōtērion* is the neuter form for safety or incidental salvation. In the main, salvation takes its distinctive meaning from that from which one is saved, and that to which and by whom he is saved. Because sin sinks us to such depths in which we are helplessly lost and penetrates to such deepest depths in human personality itself, deliverance from it is called, "so great a salvation!" And the same is true because of the heights to which salvation lifts us, by the immeasurable greatness and sacrifice of the Saviour.

2. As to how far down salvation must go to rescue the lost, we are face to face with the old expression, "total depravity." This has been taken to mean just what it says, namely, that sin has gone to the extent where nothing of good is left in human personality. This utmost degeneration or destruction, however, was not what was meant by this phrase. Total depravity meant rather *total inability* of the soul itself to return or even to seek after a Saviour or His salvation. If this expression were to be taken literally, it would mean absolute hopelessness, as we have in the condition in which they are, who have committed the sin against the Holy Spirit. God must in salvation appeal to the lost soul and with the help of "prevenient grace," as some call it; but hardly with outright "compelling

grace for the elect." If there were total depravity, grace would have nothing to appeal to or work upon in the soul to cause it to respond. Where there is no favorable interpreting content of mind, there can be no possibility of reaching the lost as persons.

This is just the difference God foresees by His omniscience, that some will respond and some will not. "Whom He foreknows (will respond) He predestinates to be conformed to the image of the Son." Foreknows because He will compel the reception of grace? No! That would be neither grace nor foreknowledge. That would be the knowledge of His (then) present intentions, which is not true foreknowledge at all. And grace by compulsion would smack of the will of a totalitarian dictator, rather than of Divine grace. God, on the other hand, would not be omniscient did He not foreknow those who would respond to His saving love. "Elect according to the foreknowledge of God," means what it says. He elects because He must plan for every life, good or bad, as far as He can. God "girded" or elected Cyrus, though he never knew God (Isa. 45:5). He planned the utmost possible good to him and by him, as God is sure to do for every soul that He knows shall come into existence. Nothing less would fit Him as God. No arbitrary favoritism can be found in the Father.

3. There are many adverse things from which one may be saved. There may be salvation from difficulty, danger, distress, enemies, sickness and death. In Ps. 25:5 David says, "For Thou art the God of my sal-

vation." In this and other psalms he speaks of many things from which he needed salvation; but the greatest salvation was from the greatest enemy, viz. that evil when he confessed, "Against Thee, even (or specially) Thee, have I sinned and done this evil in Thy sight." While in Old Testament days the saints well understood that salvation in its deepest sense was from sin and unto God, yet only in New Testament times and since then did salvation come to mean all which was intended as the word fell from the lips of Jesus Christ. We should discriminate between the dozen salvations mentioned in the New Testament by asking about each, "*Saved from what?—To what?*" "Now is our salvation nearer to us than when we (first) believed," cannot be the same salvation as in "For by hope we were saved" (Rom. 8:24 and 13:11).

VII. Forgiveness or Remission

Many wrongly suppose that remission is a stronger word than forgiveness, perhaps because of Heb. 9:22. Note carefully it was according to the Law of the Old Covenant that "apart from shedding of blood there is no remission." Some even assert, forgiveness could be with or without "atonement," while remission means that redemptive shedding of blood is obligatory or necessary. In opposition to this view it may be pointed out that the word *aphēsis* is used equally in translations for both forgiveness and remission. The verb *aphiēmi*, to send away, to let go, to remit, to forgive, is allied to the noun *aphēsis*. In the passage from Hebrews (9:22) this noun is translated remission. In at least fifty instances in the New Testament it or its cognates are translated forgiveness, forgiven, forgive. In some nine times it is translated "remit" or "remission." As Westcott suggests, the absolute use of *aphēsis* in the passage cited (9:22) is remarkable and unusual. It is not remission or forgiveness of sins or transgressions, but just release in "the broad sense." Here then, it may be, the word remission fits a bit better than would forgiveness, inasmuch it was used under the Levitical law of commandment of sacrifice.

This passage would be poor support for unconditional forgiveness or remission. The right attitude of the one to be forgiven *is always faith*, which remission implies. The whole question of amends or reparation might also be raised. Even when full reparation is made, there still remains the personal relation beyond this.

1. Our Lord rightly claimed both the power and the right to forgive men their sins. As already explained, it was the persons who were forgiven. Especially in the Epistle to the Hebrews it is unescapable that remission of sins is not only pledged but also involved when in His redemption He is both the High Priest as well as the offering. The New Covenant has the inseparable meaning of bequeathment in our Lord's testament on our behalf, and He Himself is that bequeathment. It therefore follows as the day along with the sun that the sins for which He made Himself the sacrifice unto God He is more than willing to blot out on behalf of those who being guilty of them had

repented of the same and sought in and because of Him their own personal forgiveness. This remission is genuine, not like that of those who say, "I forgive the wrong, but I will not forget it." He who blots out of existence our iniquities, surely remembers them no more against us; and what is thus blotted out cannot in itself be forgiven.

VIII. Justification and Sanctification

These two terms also belong together; there is no justification without the sequence of sanctification, and no sanctification of a saved sinner without justification preceding it. The important matter of regeneration will be discussed in the chapter dealing with Christ's impartation of Himself. We shall find righteousness and justification inseparably bound up with each other.

1. The verb to justify is *dikaioō*; the noun is *dikaiosunē*, which means also righteousness as well as justification. *Dikaiōsis* is also used, but not so frequently. In Heb. 11:7 *Dikaiosunēs* is used to express the righteousness of Noah which was according to faith (*kata pistin*). In Rom. 4:13 the same word is used to express the righteousness of Abraham by faith (*dia pisteōs*). Rom. 9:30, "The Gentiles, who followed not after righteousness, attained to righteousness, even the righteousness which is of faith (*ek pisteōs*). In Phil. 3:9, "Not having a righteousness of mine own, even that which is of the law (*ek nomou*), but that which is through faith (*dia pisteōs*) in Christ, the righteousness which is from God by (upon) faith (*epi tē pistei*)." Here we have that righteousness according to faith,

which answers to it, holds reciprocity with faith, and is the righteousness which can come from God only. Thus it is shown that salvation which is by faith in Christ and from God is paralleled by righteousness or justification by faith in Christ and from God.

2. From the foregoing passages it is evident that righteousness according to the law and justification by it proved impossible because of sin. The other righteousness better than the legal is a vital righteousness of response by faith to the sacrifice of God in Christ. This faith in another's righteousness of sacrificial love to put away sin by the Divine, God-ordered nature in that sacrificial Person who gave Himself in death for us, is faith in a righteousness on our behalf to impart its life that had passed through a sin-death in His body. Thus we are not simply acquitted, but made righteous in Him. Hence we are justified by faith uniting us to that vicarious righteousness of our Lord. No wonder that the Epistle to the Hebrews presents such an array of Faith's heroes, for it reveals both the infinite awfulness of unbelief in such a God and Saviour, and the supreme virtue of the faith of eternal life that builds its eternity upon the complete competence of the Christ as Redeemer. No one can be right with God who refuses faith in and acceptance of the Gift of the Son of His Love; and no one however weak and sinful can be basically wrong with God who takes Jesus Christ as the Divine provision of right relation to the Most High.

3. Justification is the foundation furnished on acceptance of the righteousness of Christ on our behalf.

Justification is identification with Christ by faith for growth and service. Sanctification is a sacred sort of living resulting from being set apart unto Christ. He said (John 17:19), "For their sakes I sanctify (*hagiazō*, consecrate) myself, that they themselves also may be sanctified in truth." Heb. 2:11, "For both He that sanctifieth and they that are sanctified are all of one." II Thess. 2:13, "God chose you from the beginning unto salvation in sanctification of the Spirit and belief of (faith in) the truth." Here we have mentioned the Holy Spirit as the Divine agent in sanctification. But Christ and the Holy Spirit always work together. Heb. 13:12, "Wherefore Jesus also, that He might sanctify the people through His own blood, suffered without the gate." (*Note that the first tabernacle was outside the camp.* See Exod. 33:7.) And Heb. 10:10, "By the which will we have been sanctified through the offering of the body of Christ once for all." The Father sanctified the Son: John 10:36, "Him whom the Father sanctified and sent into the world." The Father set apart or consecrated the Son to be the Saviour of the world. But this sanctification of the Son did not like that of believers rest on justification, for being eternally flawlessly perfect He needed none.

Chapter Two

THE PERSONAL VIEWPOINT IN REDEMPTION

The personal point of view is the most appropriate in the study of Redemption, because it is produced by a Person and is for persons. Every subject has its own situation which determines the vantage point for viewing it. Human personality is on earth the highest conceivable type of life with capacity for God; and the personal viewpoint is naturally like it. Human life is nothing if not personal. Because God Himself is personal in the highest conceivable order or type, He is the center and source of all our vital relations. All our vital possibilities lie within our personal relations.

The personal substance of Redemption in origin means that it is a Person who through His vicarious, sacrificial death was perfected as the means of our Redemption. He Himself said, "On the third day I am perfected." Because it is our greatest need, being redeemed from sin and death is the greatest of all our present possibilities; for He "delivered us out of so great a death, and will deliver" (II Cor. 1:10). This Hebrews 2:3 calls "so great a salvation"; and Titus 2: 13, 14 says: "Looking for the blessed hope and appearing of the glory of the great God and our Saviour Jesus Christ; who gave Himself for us, that He might redeem us from all iniquity."

1. Personality in God is first. Since personality is the highest form of living existence, in God it is the source of all other personal existences. If real personality could not be found in God, we could not explain its supreme greatness. He is that greatness of Personality we call *Absolute.* But this is a metaphysical rather than religious term. It means uncreated, self-existent, eternal, infinite, unlimited. Even absolute Personality cannot be solitary, *for the social is essential in all true personality.* The three absolute Persons in the Trinity are in absolute, that is, unlimited closeness of personal relation to each other as infinite Other-Selves. There would not be three infinities of a kind unless they were inter-existent. Whether finite or absolute, personality is essentially a thing of co-personal relations.

2. It is fortunate that God, the Trinity of absolute, counterpart Persons, was in existence before our definition of the absolute! Perhaps our definition of the absolute is not absolute in accuracy. It had better conform to what God has revealed Himself to be, rather than expect Him to conform to it; for the Absolute, if anywhere, must be in God.

No doubt these absolute inter-existences are interpersonal, as the Scriptures suggest. The infinite Father dwells in the Son, and the infinite Divine Son dwells in the Father, and the infinite Holy Spirit is in the

Father and the Son, even as They are in Him. This would be absolute personal indwelling that makes for the absolute triunity of the Trinity. So these three Absolute Persons are infinitely relative and inter-dependent. We cannot keep to the vital and personal viewpoint of the Christian faith without due regard for the invincibly inseparable Divine Three, out of Whom proceed both creation and the re-creation by Redemption.

I. Personality in God, Man, and Redemption

The first book of the Bible is appropriately named "Genesis," for it begins with God as Creator: "In the beginning God created the heavens and the earth." The Gospel of John opens with a similar beginning, that of re-creation in Redemption. But this reaches back in origin before that of creation: "In the beginning was the Word, and the Word was with God, and the Word was God. The same was in the beginning with God."

1. The personal relations in the unity of the Godhead are of primary importance. As the perfection of God proves the defection of sin to be inexcusable, so also are statements of the Trinity defective which misrepresent its unity. The two cardinal doctrines, the Godhead and Redemption, are so intertwined that when either is obscured or dropped, the other fares likewise. For this reason we must be on our guard to prevent penalistic interpretations of Redemption from ending credibility of the unity of the Trinity. It is the Trinity they sacrifice instead of witnessing to the sacrifice of Christ. Almost invariably penalists quote II Corinthians

5:21, "Him who knew no sin He made sin on our behalf." As there is never unity between God and sin, the unity between God and Christ is thought to be at an end, though the contradiction immediately appears that God cannot make sin any more than He can lie. If literally He made Christ sin, then it would not be sin, for whatever God does is right, and it would be sinless sin because God made it, for He like the Son "knows no sin."

2. This "making Christ sin" is stated in various ways. In this week's radio address a very devout evangelist quoted these words, and went on to say, "The Father made the Son sin as He hung on the cross. Then with one look He smote Him dead." No scripture says this, that the Father with one look struck the Son dead. The Word does say, "This command have I received of my Father," to submit to death "at the hands of wicked men." Acts 2:23, "Him being delivered up by the determinate counsel and foreknowledge of God, ye by the hands of lawless men did crucify and slay." Thus Peter at Pentecost expressed it. Recently a prominent preacher speaking at one of our chapel services said: "One thing I want you to remember—It was God who put Jesus Christ to death, and the wrath of God rested upon Him as He hung on the cross." How much unity of the Trinity is left by statements that God the Father murdered His own Son, as sinless as He, and who was obediently suffering the greatest iniquity that ever was perpetrated in human history? The fact is, He was sinned against, He was made sin in effect, not in cause—which was impossible.

Another radio speaker at a recent summer assembly set forth that Christ actually was made sin for us, so that He became this sin under the curse of God, and was therefore "rejected on the cross by God who turned His back upon Him." How could God make His Son sin for us, and then reject Him for being what He had made Him? With these penal interpretations we have a delirium of contradictions and absurdities with not a shred of the unity of the triune Godhead left.

Here I am not presenting what I take to be the true view of this matter. That will be taken up later on. What I am showing is that pure penalism sacrifices or abolishes the unity of the Trinity. If in any sense the Son is rejected by the Father, and instead of permitting His death, takes the main part in it, and in wrath refuses Him while in the agonies of the crucifixion, turning His back upon Him, then the unity of the Trinity ceases to have meaning in such situation and personal relation.

In case some are impatient and demand at once what Christ thought and said about His relations to the Father during His passion, here it is: "Therefore doth my Father love me because I lay down my life, that I may take it again. No one taketh it away from me, but I lay it down of myself. I have power to lay it down, and I have power to take it again. This commandment received I of my Father" (John 10: 17, 18).

3. The Word of God, when wisely interpreted and not plucked out in disjointed passages, presents harmonious statements of the Trinity in Redemption. Then

we find the Scriptures are inspired by that Holy Spirit of living correspondence with Him who is the Truth in the realm of Divine expression as to the Persons of the Godhead and their inseparable interexistence and interrelations, and their goings forth to bring men to God and into the infinite outreach of life eternal.

The matchless, incomparable unity of the Trinity is grounded in the preëminent and perfect character of the Persons composing it. In the Godhead there can be no "make-and-break" unity. All the powers of sin and hell are not able to disrupt the eternal relations of the Trinity. Since our Redemption has its source and substance in the personal unity of the Godhead, the necessity is apparent that it should be presented from the personal viewpoint. An objection to the penal point of view is that it is artificially legal and not primarily personal and vital. Having been made in the personal image and likeness of God, man did not and could not lose his personal order of existence even when sin came upon him, and he broke away from God. See Gen. 5:1; Phil. 2:7.

4. Defining Redemption as *the Divine Restoration of human persons to right relation to God and to each other*, gives the personal point of view the highest adaptation to and correspondence with the nature of our subject. What personality is in both God and man is in this way made manifest. We may also define Personality as *the highest conceivable type of life and the highest imaginable order of existence.* Some define the Divine as super-personal, holding that it transcends personality altogether as we know it. But this over-

shoots the mark, for it makes the Divine impersonal to us, because there is then not a single power, characteristic, or attribute which can be named as belonging to the super-personal, which thus becomes the super-knowable. In God's revelation of Himself in Holy Writ His personality is not thus set forth. There He is not presented as the Great Unknown and Unknowable.

Defining more fully life itself we may say, *it is correspondence, reciprocity, or intercourse with adapted, kindred, counterpart or interacting environment.* When set forth as utterly transcending this conception of life, we have neither life nor personality. The rank of both depends upon the rank of their kindred environment. Absolute Personality must have absolute correspondence with the absolute in kind, that is, the infinite. And there cannot be more than one infinite of a kind unless in complementary inter-existence. The three Persons of the Trinity are complementary co-absolutes and inter-existent. They are more than co-personal. They are inter-personal inter-existences. Such life is other-conscious and sacrificial in the highest possible extent and inter-relation. The Trinity has within itself its own personal environment. Later on we shall discuss this matter further.

5. *Essential to all personal life is the co-personal or social relation.* Reciprocity in social relation is indispensable to it. Hence the Unitarian God as one solitary Personality is either unsocial and thus defective, or if social, is without the necessary counterpart correspondence. If He must create to provide companionship—satisfaction for His social nature, He ceases to be abso-

lute. How could He have social reciprocity not in keeping with Himself as Uncreated Being? Here the Absolute is bound to require the co-absolute *socius.* Hence God *is either impersonal or more than one person.*

The social relation of man with man is the co-personal. This comes from mankind being a race. In God the social is much closer, for each of the Three Persons is inseparable from the other two. The Persons of the Godhead are constitutionally involved with each other in inter-existence. So the triunity of the Trinity is vastly higher, deeper, stronger and greater than human unity of persons at their best. In fact, our unity with one another has to be in God, or it does not go very deep or very far. It is out of the Great Resources of the Divine Triunity that Redemption came forth to save us from the disunity of iniquity.

6. Life being essentially a thing of the highest order of relations and activities, it cannot be well considered apart from them. As already suggested, the God-Life has its own vital relations of life eternal in the Trinity. These relations are expressed in mutual and perfect self-giving of faith, love, sacrifice and full coöperation. As there is mutual complementing in social relations, so in the Godhead there is absolute or infinite environment of kindred or counterpart personality in the highest order of mutual and complementary correspondence or reciprocity, of which we can conceive.

Each Divine Person in being related to man carries into this relation His Divine inter-relations with all their fulness, resources and sufficiency of the interpersonal relation of the Trinity. In the Trinity there are the two orders of unity, that within each Divine Person, and that between the Three Divine Persons. Out of the vast resources of the unity of the Trinity came the riches of Redemption to displace the disunity of sin in human life.

7. According to Colossians 1:15 and 3:10 it was in *the image of the Son* in which God made man; and this creation thereby constituted God the highest Environment and the only Source of man's spiritual life. Man was thus integrated into living relations to the highest order of personality and unity. The disaster of sin broke away human life and made Redemption indispensable. *This is our point of view of Redemption.* This vital statement of it may be difficult to some. To comprehend Divine Personality and the Divine life in unity cannot be other than hard for the strongest human minds. When the Divine, the Infinite and the Absolute are made easy, it is only by making them empty. Our vital point of view is in the midst of the embarrassment of riches in the Divine-human personality of the Incarnate Son of God.

II. Redemption in Godward and Manward Aspects

The Godward and the manward aspects of Redemption have long been looked upon as covering this subject. They are sometimes called the Making and the Mediation of Christ's sacrifice for us. Inseparably they are complementary views. The Godward naturally has precedence because casual, instrumental and fontal.

While the three Persons of the Godhead participated in Redemption, the Son is the central figure because He is the Divine Sacrifice in Person. He holds the center of the stage, so to speak, throughout both aspects of Redemption; and will so continue until its consummation in the *Parousia* or Second Coming of our Lord.

Within the Person of God the Son there are most wonderful possibilities of *becoming*. "The Word *became* flesh, and dwelt among us; (and we beheld His glory, glory as of the only begotten from the Father), full of grace and truth." But verse eighteen in the Prologue of John's Gospel has the most astounding expression of all as to His possibilities of *becoming*: "God only-begotten," or "Only-begotten God," (*monogenēs Theos*). (See margin A. R. V., John 1:18.) Even with the transcendent viewpoint of Divine Personality we are sure to find these personal possibilities in the Godhead bring into the subject of Redemption implications and outreaches so immeasurable, they beggar human language in attempting to portray their fulness of meaning and far-reaching results.

This opening chapter of John's Gospel goes on to say: "For of His fulness have we all received, and grace for grace" (i.e., grace upon grace). In Col. 1: 19, 20 Paul says, "It pleased the Father that in Him (the Son) should all the fulness dwell (or, the whole fulness of God was pleased to dwell in Him); and through Him to reconcile all things unto Himself, having made peace through the blood of His cross; through Him, I say, whether things upon the earth or things in the heavens."

1. When interpreting the Bethlehem birth we need to use the transcendent personal point of view, and explain the Incarnation by what the preëxistent Son became by it. We propose to do a similar thing in interpreting His death by what He became by it; for in what Christ *became* by His sacrifice on the cross there is excellent exposition or explanation of *the very heart and soul of His Redemption,* which is not so much a work as it is a Person.[5] "*He* is the propitiation for our sins." "The Heart of the New Testament" is profoundly personal.

The sacrifice of His birth made possible the sacrifice of His death. As II Cor. 8:9 puts it, "Though He was rich, yet for your sakes He became poor that ye through His poverty might become rich." In the sacrifice by emptying (*kenosis*) Himself, He left behind His place or rank (*morphe*) as God. Phil. 2:7 shows how He took the place or rank (*morphe,* again) of a bond-slave, *becoming* obedient unto death, even the death of the cross. Here the verb *kenoō* cannot mean that He emptied Himself of Himself. That was impossible, for He was still Himself though in deep abnegation. For the time being He had forsaken His own place and its privileges, His honor and glory as the Son in heaven.

2. The Incarnation was a sacrifice so great, some have considered it, rather than His death, as our Redemption. The Scriptures, however, uniformly set forth Christ's sacrifice of Himself by His death on the cross

[5] In John 17:4 Jesus said before His crucifixion, "I have finished the work which thou gavest me to do." Nowhere does He call His sacrifice in death a work.

as His personal process of becoming to redeem mankind. As I Peter 1: 18-21 states it, "Ye were not redeemed with corruptible things, as silver and gold . . . but with the precious blood of Christ as of a lamb without blemish and without spot: who verily was foreordained before the foundation of the world, but was manifest in these last times for you, who by Him do believe in God, that raised Him up from the dead, and gave Him glory; that your faith and hope might be in God." That is the glorious culmination of the Process.

III. Christ's Death Better than Atonement

In this chapter it may be fitting to notice also that in the entire New Testament the word "Redemption" and its cognate terms replace the Old Testament term "Atonement." When we come to the study of the Epistle of the Hebrews, we find that Atonement wholly belonged to the First or Old Covenant, and Redemption has place in the better, the New Covenant. *The theme of this Epistle is,* Christ's sacrifice is in every way *better* than the sacrifices of the blood of beasts offered under the Levitical Covenant, while Christ offered Himself to God by His shed blood of the New Covenant. It is no wonder then that the inspiration of the Holy Spirit in the Scriptures passes up the old term "Atonement," referring to the sacrifices of the blood of beasts "which could never take away sin." When the Son of God offered up Himself unto God to take away sin, this "more excellent sacrifice" is described in the *better terms* of the New Testament or Covenant.

1. The English word "Atonement" means at-one-ment or reconciliation, while the Hebrew word *kipper* or *kopher*, it is supposed to translate, means "covering." Those who make the verb *kaphar*, to cover, mean to reconcile, forget that the Old Testament would have to be written first in English to have the word "atonement" so used. The eminent Old Testament scholar, Prof. A.B. Davidson, has raised the question whether it is sin or the eyes of God that is covered in atonement. In any case it is God, and not the blood of sacrifice, which does the covering; and this covering is in but *a metaphorical sense*. Dr. Davidson says: "Jehovah does not first atone or cover the sin, and then follow this by forgiveness; the atoning or covering is merely a figure for forgiveness. It might be that *kipper* in the sense of forgive was a secondary usage, derived from the primary sense of to *cover* or *atone*, either by a life ransom or a sacrifice; and that the sense "forgive" was properly *to declare atoned for*." [6]

IV. The Scriptures True to the Personal Viewpoint

In setting forth Redemption the Scriptures faithfully maintain the personal point of view. In Ephesians 1:7 the Person of Christ is emphasized: "In whom (Jesus Christ) we have our redemption through His blood, the forgiveness of our trespasses, according to the riches of His grace, wherewith He abounded toward us . . . to sum up all things in Christ." Rom. 3:24 says, "Being justified freely by His grace through the

[6] **Theology of the Old Testament, p. 329.**

redemption that is in Christ Jesus." Similarly also in Col. 1: 13-17, "Who delivered us out of the power of darkness, and translated us into the kingdom of the Son of His love; *in Whom* we have our redemption, the forgiveness of our sins: who is the image of the invisible God, the firstborn of all creation; for *in Him* were all things created . . . all things have been created *through Him and unto Him; and He is before all things, and in Him all things hold together*" (*sunistēmi*).

1. Taking another cognate term used with Redemption, that of "Propitiation," we have the same emphasis on Christ in Person. It is well to note first that properly it is wrath, anger or indignation of a person which may be propitiated. *In no place in the New Testament does it say that the death of Christ propitiated God.* Invariably it is Christ Himself who is or becomes this propitiation. I John 2:2 says, "He is the propitiation for our sins, and not for ours only, but for the sins of the whole world." In I John 4:10 we are told God loved us, "and sent His Son to be the propitiation for our sins." In each of these passages, as already noted, the word for propitiation is *hilasmos.* In Romans 3:25 Paul uses a similar word, *hilastērion,* which the Septuagint uses for mercy-seat, the place of propitiation. "Through the redemption that is in Christ Jesus; whom God hath set forth to be a propitiation through faith in His blood." This is an important qualification, "through faith in His blood." The inspired writer of the Epistle to the Hebrews says of Christ in chapter

2:17: "Wherefore it behooved Him in all things to be made like unto His brethren, that He might become a merciful and faithful high priest in things pertaining to God, to make propitiation for the sins of the people." Here *hilaskomai,* in the present infinitive, *hilaskesthai* with *eis* is used in the reflexive middle voice, meaning to the end of, to become, to be, or to make Himself propitiation, as Christ was both High Priest as well as the offering. The present tense points to the everlasting perpetuation of propitiation. Some translate it "to make expiation," to remove guilt.

2. Why and how does Christ become propitiation? In His perfect righteousness of absolute holiness, God cannot be other than infinitely indignant with iniquity. As this anger is unconditional as long as sin exists, and absolutely nothing in any degree can make sin agreeable to Him, *one thing alone* can allay His indignation or quench His wrath, and that is *the cessation of sin's existence.* This we have already discussed. If our blessed Lord had died a thousand times with no provision to secure iniquity's extermination, God's anger with it must have gone on just the same.

Because through His death the Son of God had become the efficient or effectual means to blot out sin from human lives, to exterminate it from human persons, He is said to be the propitiation for our sins. John states the method of this eradication, which we shall study further later on. I John 1:7, "The blood of Jesus His Son cleanseth (literally, keeps on cleansing) us from all sin." Just what is meant by the cleansing blood of Christ, and "Redemption in His blood" is of deep interest and will also be inquired into later on. This, however, is now clear, that since sin is immeasurably hateful to God, unchangeably repugnant to Him, and absolutely damnable, the only possible way His holy anger with it can be done away, is by doing away with it. This is Christ's *great Success as a Saviour*, that He ends the part and place of iniquity in human lives, stops its pernicious agency in anti-God personal realization, ends it as the accursed cause of Godward barrenness, selfishness and enmity.

3. From what we have found we may conclude that God readily forgives sinners, but *never forgives sin*. Any scriptural expression that He forgives sin really means that He forgives the persons who sin, once they repent of their sin. To speak of forgiving sin could only be metonymy for pardoning sinners. In itself iniquity is altogether unforgivable. As previously quoted, Doctor Fairbairn has said, "There is something infinite about sin."[7] Yes, for it is infinitely unreasonable, infinitely accursed, infinitely inexcusable, infinitely unforgivable.

[7] The Place of Christ in Modern Theology, p. 453.

Chapter Three

BLOOD THE SYMBOL OF SACRIFICE

Introduction

In the Scriptures from their beginning blood is regarded as sacred and the emblem of sacrifice. Because it lacked blood and faith that worked obedience, Cain's sacrifice was not accepted of God. He kept the blood of his herds but was not slow to shed upon the ground his brother's blood. The Lord said unto him: "The voice of thy brother's blood crieth unto me from the ground." Hebrews 11:4, "By faith Abel offered unto God a more excellent sacrifice than Cain." Heb. 12:24, "To Jesus the mediator of the New Covenant, and to the blood of sprinkling, that speaketh better things than that of Abel." Abel's shed blood accused, and righteously so; but the blood of sprinkling, *Christ's blood of the New Covenant,* spoke peace and redemption, and that in righteousness. Evidently sacrificial worship from the beginning had been instituted by God, and directions doubtless were given as to what the offering for sin should be; for Abel would hardly have selected the right offering by mere chance.

1. In Genesis 9:4 we find the first scripture telling of the prohibition of blood for food. This direction was to Noah and his sons. The first seventeen chapters of Leviticus contain extended account of the sacrificial offerings required; and here again we find the use of blood for food forbidden because of its sacred character. "The life of the flesh is in the blood; and I have given it unto you upon the altar to make atonement for your souls; for it is the blood that maketh atonement for the soul. . . . No soul of you shall eat blood, neither shall any stranger that sojourneth among you eat blood. . . . For the life of all flesh is the blood thereof."

2. Because human life is above all other life on earth, human blood was regarded as the most sacred of all. The human body would be counted likewise sacred. In Paul's great classic on the Resurrection are found the memorable words: "All flesh is not the same flesh: but there is one kind of flesh of men, another flesh of beasts, another of fishes, and another of birds." "It is written, The first Adam was made a living soul." While God made body and blood, soul and spirit, human life is transmitted by generation, but not the blood; the human embryo forms its own blood. By the union of conception or epi-genesis the two cells unite with their genes and chromosomes. In development the heart is first formed, then the large blood-vessels like the aorta, then the blood itself.

I. The Scriptures' Account of the Incarnation

To the question, "Where did Jesus get His blood?" the usual answer is: "From His mother, Mary." This is not quite accurate. To "the seed of the woman" there was added by the Holy Spirit the Supernatural Life. More than that, this conception was by the Holy Ghost, we do not know, even as we are utterly unable to explain the process of any miracle; and the Incarnation was the miracle of all miracles. There is more of the supernatural and unknown in it than in any other miracle, except perhaps the Resurrection of Christ. How a preëxistent Divine Person by the help of the other two inter-existent Persons of the Trinity could be conceptually united to the genital life from Mary, no one but God knows and understands. We should recognize that the finite human nature was added to the Divine and Infinite in the preëxistent Person of the Son. Perhaps it is not too much to say that the human-Divine embryo took its place somewhat within the center of the infinite and eternal Son's Person. How the infinite could be incarnate in or with the finite, we are a long way from knowing.

1. Lacking the necessary omniscience to explain this mystery of mysteries, we may (yea, we must) rest in the fact that this great Personal union of the supernatural with the natural amply verified itself in the sinless Son of God, Life and Person coming forth from or through it. This result revealed the measure and character of the cause or antecedents. Mere human heredity is wholly insufficient to explain that absolutely perfect and purely sinless life of the incomparable, sacrificial Person. For mere or purely human origin to produce the Christ life, character and personality would be harder to explain than the adequate miracle

of the Incarnation. That is evidently adequate supernatural cause. Purely and solely natural human cause for this most marvelous incomparable effect is as incongruous as inadequate. To believe that there was direct, special interposition of God not only in means but in substance would be far more reasonable than the flat contradiction between visible effect and hopelessly insufficient cause to explain it. Surely it is far better to have adequate origin or cause in or by the Supernatural in the Persons of the Trinity without full explanation of its way of working, than to have this tremendous effect or result linked to utterly unbelievable source, that is, to infinitely disproportionate means.

2. One of the most ancient creeds says, "He was conceived of the Holy Ghost, born of the Virgin Mary." Any other view adds vastly more difficulty than it would exclude. The supernaturally fertilized ovum was in consequence as different from an ordinary human embryo as the added Divine Life itself was different. And the blood formed by this altogether unique embryo represented extraordinary and unprecedented life, and *differed from ordinary human blood accordingly,* for "the blood is the life"; and His life was infinitely more than human life. By as much as the Son of God and Son of man was different from and superior to all other men, so also was His blood. It was "richer blood" than theirs, for it had all the tremendous significance and divine sacredness of His Incarnation. When that blood was shed, it was the blood of the Godman, the blood of a Divine-human body. By that blood the Son

of God was able to live in this world, to live His life along with ours. Physically, the blood of Christ was the instrumental means of the life of the Incarnation. To shed it was to drive out the Son of God from living a human life among the sons of men.

3. Of course, anti-supernaturalists refuse to credit the Incarnation, just as they deny also Christ's Deity, His miracles, His redeeming death, His resurrection, and power to give the Holy Spirit; for only God can give the Spirit of God. In such denial of the supernatural practically the whole of vital Christianity is at stake. What unbelieving naturalism would leave is nothing more than the infinitely less important fragments of it without power of redemption, and with none of the essentials of Divine Nature and Personality.

4. We should recognize that the Incarnation was not an afterthought with God. To Omniscience nothing can be afterthought. In the beginning human nature was made great enough, and was closely enough related to admit of the Word being made flesh. When man was created in the image and likeness of God, the foundational possibility on the human side was provided for *so that the Incarnation could take place.* For that original creation was in the very likeness of the supernatural, even the supernatural God Himself. This on man's side clearly gave him capacity for God and definite affinity with the supernatural. And on the Divine side it gave the Son not only the relation of Creator, breathing into man the breath of His life, but also of

shaping and moulding man's very spirit with capacity to be a son of God.

5. To make Redemption really possible, there could be no other point at which the supernatural so fully and so personally related Itself to us as in the Incarnation. In fact there is nothing which God has done that is explained fully or finally in process; so that the Incarnation does not stand alone as not fully explained in process. That He has not explained the unexplainable by reason of our finite capacity in understanding how the preëxistent Person united human nature and life to His Divine nature and life, does not prohibit the potent, patent fact of this from being accepted. If men will not receive this fact of the Supernatural Conception, neither will they be likely to receive the Supernatural Redemption for which it prepared the way. If the whole of the Supernatural is taken to be unbelievable, then God Himself, His creation of man, and His Redemption for mankind are likewise to be classed as incredible.

6. The Christ Himself in coming to us also revealed most clearly this great fact of the Divine plan of supernatural Redemption. This He did in His natural as well as supernatural Person and Life, to say nothing of His transparent teaching on the subject. We should also note that wherever God is pleased to join Himself to us in the close personal relation of identification, both the natural and the supernatural are necessarily linked together in the life-process resulting therefrom.

Inevitably, then, the greater and closer this identification of all such conjoining of the Divine with human life, the greater must be the mystery in the movements of its processes. The only way to avoid the palpable mystery is to refuse Christianity or to stop thinking. The naturalism which objects to all the supernatural is surely not as sacred and valuable and saving as it. And naturalism itself is not without its own mysteries and far more unsolvable than those of supernaturalism. What sort of redemption has it to offer in place of that of Christ? To be consistent it has no God at all, unless Nature is taken to be such.

This mystery of the Incarnation is the mark and the measure of what God did, and in which He was vitally and personally present. Job 11:7 says, "Canst thou by searching find out God? Canst thou find out the Almighty unto perfection?" And Isaiah 40:28 tells us, "The everlasting God, Jehovah, the Creator of the ends of the earth . . . there is no searching of His understanding." And the Apostle Peter tells us in his First Epistle, 1: 10, 11, "Concerning which salvation (the end of your faith) the prophets sought and searched diligently, who prophesied of the grace that should come unto you; searching what time or what manner of time the Spirit of Christ which was in them did point unto, when it testified beforehand the sufferings of Christ, and the glories that should follow." Paul begins in I Tim. 3:16 a list of the mysteries along with that of the Incarnation: "Great is the mystery of godliness, God was manifest in the flesh." By this all the rest of the Divine manifestations became possible in Redemption.

II. Blood Constitutionally Sacrificial

Some persons unfortunately cultivate disgust toward all blood, regarding it as coarse, repulsive and gruesome. The wonder is that they carry it about with them everywhere. Having such disgust for it, why do they not replace it with ice-water in their arteries and veins? But some cannot help taking fright at the sight of blood. This abnormal aversion may be completely conquered by giving or receiving blood in transfusion. When thus a life has been saved, the blood naturally comes into high regard as a saving thing. When the sacrificial nature of the blood is studied, and our debt to it understood, it is not difficult to esteem it according to its great service to human life.

1. Histology is that branch of biology which treats of the structure of the tissues of organized, that is, living bodies. The functions and character of these bodies are most interesting. Human blood is made up first of all of a fluid, plasma, or lymph, in which varied corpuscles swim or are carried along in the current of circulation. Each type of these tiny bodies has its own specific task. By far the most numerous are the red ones, some five million in a single drop of blood. They are mainly sacs of hemoglobin which carry oxygen from the lungs to all parts of the body. When worn out they are transported to the liver and turned into bile. The leucocytes are living sacrifices to protect the body from enemy bacteria. These corpuscles are of various forms and have different ways of carrying on their war. Some are stationed guards like an officer

on the street corner. Some are roving guards like motorcycle policemen. When they discover enemy bacteria in the lungs, for example, they surround the foe and ingest it and feed upon it. They have a most uncanny way of becoming aware when and where in the body that infection by hostile bacteria is at work. Automatically they multiply to meet the need and flock to the place where the trouble is. A blood-count is usually of these leucocytes to find out from their number that which it automatically indicates, whether there is infection somewhere in the body. The lymphocytes are another type of corpuscle. They oil the joints, feed the nerves, remove fatigue toxins, and carry off to the liver the defunct red corpuscles. These are some but not all the types of toilers in the blood.

The temperature of the body is controlled by the blood. It carries the food elements to where they are needed in nourishment, growth and rebuilding. In fact most all the needs arising out of the internal conditions and external labor of the body are ministered unto by the blood. This brief and imperfect summary is intended to call attention to the function and nature of the blood in its many-sided sacrificial services rendered to human life by it. It is because of the place the blood occupies that it became the insignia of sacrifice in life and religion. Evidently God in His great wisdom when planning the nature, function and place of the blood, took the pattern of it from things spiritual in which the sacrificial is paramount.

2. Life is essentially spiritual in nature even when

related to or integrated in the physical world. No number of physical terms adequately or competently describe life's phases, its correspondences, intercourses, intelligent reciprocities, and other factors. The blood itself is spiritual as far as it is life, and it is the means of relating, designating and integrating human life in this physical universe. His blood enabled Jesus Christ to live as an inhabitant of this physical world.

Since the blood is the relating and designating agent which makes the human soul belong to this world, the shedding of it ends its life in relation to the physical order. When for any reason or cause the sacrificial service of the blood comes to an end, the body dies and the soul departs, or is thus disembodied. When Christ's blood was poured out until His heart broke and was no longer able to send the blood coursing through His arteries and veins, He passed out of this world into the world of spirit. So the life-giving service of the blood stands between our bodies and their disintegration, just as the sacrifice of our Redeemer stands between us and spiritual death.

3. Because His blood functioned in this integral relation to His bodily life in this physical world, it has been used in the Scriptures and elsewhere as the insignia of Christ's sacrifice in His Incarnation, Death and Redemption. On account of the essentially or constitutionally sacrificial character of the blood-life, His blood has become the appropriate symbol of what the Son of God became to us by the two great sacrifices of His birth and His death. The blood of His Incarna-

tion body is the Divine-human emblem representing what God is to us in and by Him. It points straight to His Spirit in His being made bone of our bone and flesh of our flesh, for His blood was the living bond which invisibly held together His Deity united with His humanity bound up together in a human body. But the most important pointing or directing of the blood is straight to the sacrifice of His life to destroy sin through His death on the cross, which fitted Him so to do. Here it is once more recognized as the great institutive agent and power and factor in the Redemptive effect in perfecting the Christ both as the Offering and our High Priest, as the Epistle to the Hebrews expresses it. In a word, the shedding of His precious blood instituted and completed or perfected Him as our great sacrifice for sins forever. There the Incarnation Body became the gateway picture of the outpouring of His Redeeming Life, not only for, but also into, human lives and persons. Later we propose to show that His Risen Body has still a place in imparting Christ in the Redemption of man personally, for the Great High Priest in the Heavenly Holy of Holies in the immediate presence of God "ever liveth to make intercession for us."

III. The Blood of Christ in the Bible

Since Christ's blood is the insignia, token and symbol of the sacrificial, redeeming love of God in Him, we should regard it accordingly. This may be overdone, or the reverse. The blood apart from the Lord Himself may be taken as that which redeems. A man in describing the crucifixion and the value of the blood, said: "If by chance a drop of the Saviour's blood dropped on one of the Roman soldier's hands as he was driving the nails through Christ's hands or feet, that pagan soldier would be instantly saved." There are those who thus materialize the spiritual, and those who spiritualize the physical. Both lead to erroneous conclusions. When the wafer is supposed to be turned into the very substance of the Son of God (transubstantiation), that is spiritualizing the physical. When water is blessed to turn it into "holy water," that is materializing the spiritual. The blood of Jesus Christ as a symbol of His sacrificial, saving power is well so regarded; but the blood completely changed from insignia to its substance of redeeming efficacy is not so good. It is worthy of note how the Scriptures use and do not abuse the figure as primal fact, the symbol as the substance, the emblem as the sacrifice of Christ Himself.

1. Let us beware of going to the other extreme of considering the blood of Christ as symbol only. The flag of our country is a symbol of it; but it is not a vital part of the country as blood is of a human body, to say nothing of an Incarnation body. We could change our flag, but not our blood. The blood of our Lord was not only a token of the sacrifice of Himself: it was a living, vital part of Him, a part of that Redeeming sacrifice in being shed, when "His soul was poured out unto death." For example, Christ as the Lamb of God is a sacrificial figure of speech;

but His actual blood is no mere figure. It is patent, vital fact in a way that figure is not. As a drop of it is a sample of blood, so the blood of Christ was a sacrificial sample of the Incarnate Person of our Lord. For this reason when the blood of Christ is used as an expression, never does it mean just the blood alone when referring to His redemption from sin. *"His blood" is the poetic, personal, sacrificial, vital expression of Christ's self-giving in Redemption.* It is spiritual as well as physical, for the life is spirit.

2. I Peter 1:19 speaks of "the precious blood, as of a lamb without blemish and without spot, even the blood of Christ" (R.V.). Some dislike the expression, "the precious blood." They would not object to it when referring to a beloved mother or a precious child of their own. The Holy Spirit is the Author of all delicacy that is devout, as we find in the Word of God. Ps. 72:14 says, "And precious will their blood be in His sight." This, by the way, is the blood of the poor and needy. If that blood is precious in God's sight because their lives are precious unto Him, how much more precious must the redeeming blood of the Lamb of God be Who "beareth away the sin of the world," as John the Baptist said. Think also of the attitude of those whose loved ones were saved from death by the Passover blood: Exod. 12:13, "And the blood shall be to you for a token upon the house where ye are: and when I see the blood I will pass over you." In I Cor. 5:7 we read, "For our passover also hath been sacrificed, even Christ." In Heb. 10:

27-30 there is a passage dealing with apostasy from Redemption by Divine grace which shows the way inspiration looks upon it in terms of the covenant blood: "Of how much sorer punishment, think ye, shall he be judged worthy, who hath trodden under foot the Son of God, and hath counted the blood of the covenant wherewith he was sanctified an unholy (common) thing, and hath done despite unto the Spirit of Grace?" In Acts 20:28 we read, "Feed the church of God which He (God) hath purchased with His own blood."

3. While we have not as yet come in our discussion to the interpretation and significance of the spiritual transfusion of the redeeming blood of Christ, the loosing, washing and cleansing by it, we may in passing say, the figure of the blood used in many ways belongs generically to Oriental symbolism. The Bible is oriental in its language. Eastern people are gifted with stronger imagination than that of the Western. We would hardly ever say, "All the trees of the fields shall clap their hands"; nor would we say, "Let him with a stick of timber in his eye not try to take a speck of dust out of his brother's eye." In Rev. 17:6, "I saw the woman drunken with the blood of the saints, and with the blood of the martyrs of Jesus." Earlier in Rev. 14:19, 20, "The great winepress of the wrath of God. And the winepress was trodden without the city, and there came out blood from the winepress, even unto the bridles of the horses, as far as a thousand and six hundred furlongs." That is two hundred miles.

4. Turning back to the earlier teaching of Christ, when speaking of full reception of Himself as Saviour

He said as recorded in John 6:52-56, "Except ye eat the flesh of the Son of man and drink His blood, ye have not life in yourselves. He that eateth my flesh and drinketh my blood hath eternal life, and I will raise him up at the last day. For my flesh is true food indeed, and my blood is true drink indeed. He that eateth my flesh and drinketh my blood abideth in me, and I in him." Concerning proper partaking of the Lord's Supper it was said in I Cor. 11:27, "Wherefore whosoever shall eat of the bread or drink of the cup of the Lord in an unworthy manner, shall be guilty of the body and of the blood of the Lord." This reminds us of Ps. 51:14, "Deliver me from bloodguiltiness, O God, Thou God of my salvation!" There is evidently more than one way of being bloodguilty. To refuse utterly and with complete aversion turn away from the Biblical blood-language, is to be blind to its truth because not stated in just our own Western way. It seems that for us the more important a truth, the more we desire the statement of it apart from all figure, symbol and metaphor; that is, in our matter of fact Western way. For the Eastern mind the reverse is nearer its way. The more important the truth the more it turns to the very strongest metaphors, figures and symbols, and the brighter the colors in which the Eastern mind paints it. What we prefer as our mode of statement is one thing: how we interpret the thought of the Eastern mind from its own language, is decidedly another. H. Clay Trumbull in his valuable work on "The Blood Covenant" says:

"Then it was, also, that the prayer of Jesus for His new blood-covenant friends went up: 'Father, the hour is come; glorify Thy Son, that the Son may glorify Thee; even as Thou gavest Him authority over all flesh, that whatsoever (whomsoever) Thou hast given Him, to them He should give eternal life (in an eternal covenant of blood) . . .'

"It was not an utterly new symbolism that Jesus was introducing into the religious thought of the world: it was rather a new meaning that he was introducing into or he was disclosing in, an already widely recognized symbolism. The world was familiar with the shadow of truth; Jesus now made clear to the world the truth's substance. Man's longing to be a partaker of the divine nature had manifested itself through all the ages and everywhere . . . (He) 'brought life and immortality to light through the gospel' of his blood-covenant.

"But a covenant of blood, a covenant to give one's blood, one's life, for the saving of another, cannot be consummated without the death of the covenanter. 'For where (such) a covenant is, there must of necessity be (be brought) the death of him that made it. For (such) a covenant is of force (becomes a reality) where there hath been death (or, over the dead): for doth it (such a covenant) ever avail (can it be efficient) while he that made it liveth.' " [8]

"To give this blood, the giver himself must die; but it was his blood, his life, not his death, which was to be the means of cure." [9]

This reminds us of what is said in Rom. 5:10: "For if, while we were enemies, we were reconciled to God through the death of His Son, much more, being reconciled, shall we be saved *by His life.*"

With this should go the preceding verse: "Much more then, being now justified by His blood, shall we be saved from the wrath (of God) through Him."

[8] **The Blood Covenant,** p. 283 ff. Second Edition. John D. Wattles, Philadelphia, Pa.
[9] Ibid., p. 287.

Chapter Four

THE PERSON AND THE PRIESTHOOD OF CHRIST

Introduction

To master the subject of "The Heart of the New Testament" in Divine Redemption is no easy task. Its phases are many; and all the great doctrines of Christianity converge upon it. There are great depths and heights to it. The doctrine upon which it most depends is that of the Trinity. Some so-called theories of Redemption really make the doctrine of the triune Godhead impossible. Men have certain pet ideas; when these are not incorporated in a statement of Christ's death, they refuse all else no matter how worthy. But this doctrine is of primary importance, because Redemption is supreme in value. No system of Christian doctrine is really strong, if weak at its center in *the statement of all statements,* the explanation of what Christ is to us because of what He has become for us. This in turn depends on the doctrine of His Person.

1. The Epistle to the Hebrews, like the Gospel of John, begins with an appraisal of the Person of the Son of God. Like John and Paul, all the other New

Testament writers who mention it, particularly the author of Hebrews, alike accept without argument the personal preëxistence and Deity of God the Son.

This Epistle is perhaps the purest in theological form in all the Scriptures. As many have noticed, its theme or key word is "better." There is the better covenant, the better promises, the better Mediator, the better sacrifice, the better hope, the better High Priest in better sanctuary, better than the angels, better than Moses and the Aaronic priesthood, and even than Melchizedek, the better country desired, the better possession, the better resurrection, and finally the blood of Jesus speaking better than that of Abel.

That this Epistle is specially adapted to the Jewish mind is easy to discern. But it is helpful to all Christians, though the great aim of the writer is to prevent Hebrew Christians from backsliding, from sinking into the apostasy of throwing overboard altogether the Christian faith, hope and assurance. For this reason we have doctrine and exhortation coupled with admonition alternating all the way through.

2. After showing the superiority of Christ over the angels, and the historical setting of the sacrifices of the Levitical law, therefrom the writer builds up to the everlasting climax of the great sacrifice in and by Christ as High Priest in the heavenly sanctuary and Holy of Holies. This leads one to make a general appraisal of the Old Testament as containing a vast fund of information indispensable to a full understanding of very many of the teachings of the New Testament. This is especially applicable in the matter of

Divine Redemption through faith in the sacrifice of Christ.

The Hebrew mind like some others has "the defects of its qualities." Its intense monotheism may refuse the higher monotheism of the Christian faith. It has refused to accept the fact that God is One in the Christian view as truly as in the Hebrew. This is mainly because the Jewish mind stumbles at the Deity of Christ, as though it meant that a man became God, instead of God becoming man.

The Writer of the Epistle to the Hebrews had the veil removed from his mind, as Paul expressed it, and this had saved him from the barren Unitarianism in which most Jews remain unto this day. What would he have thought of the maudlin Modalism which is a disguised return to Unitarianism? In this Epistle the thought swings out into the vast open and up to the infinite and eternal in the reality of Divine Redemption, and into the Deity of Christ which must accompany it, as well as surround it.

3. The Epistle to the Hebrews is unique in giving the very important aspect of the New Covenant in its double meaning of compact and bequeathment. This interpretation does not lend itself to superficial theories of Redemption. As we have seen, it presents the Son as the substance of this compact, and Christ imparting Himself by the Holy Spirit as Re-Creator (in regeneration) and His indwelling by the Holy Spirit as the bequeathment realizing Christlikeness, faith, love, service and steadfastness. The same unique-

ness may be observed all through the presentation of the sublime High Priesthood of Christ offering up Himself as the personal sacrifice holy, well-pleasing and acceptable to God. Christ as this High Priest could hardly be penalized or penalize Himself in either of these phases of offering Himself to God or as bequeathment to man. The writer shows no consciousness of having left out any essential element in the completeness of that sacrifice—for man's redemption. One could challenge Penalists to find a solitary line of support in all the Epistle to the Hebrews.

I. The Person of Christ

There are certain things in this Epistle to the Hebrews and in other New Testament Scriptures about the Person of Christ which are central, strategic and fundamental facts in vital Christianity. The same One Who is the Living Logos, a Person in the Godhead, is also the New Covenant High Priest and Divine Sacrifice. He is God in expression and the Word thereof. He is the Truth of God and the Speaker of it. He is God's Message and the Messenger. He brings the Gospel and He is the Gospel. He is both Redeemer and our Redemption. As John has said, He is "the only-begotten God" "manifest in the flesh" (John 1:18, marg.).

It was through Him that God made the worlds (ages). He is the effulgence of the Divine glory, the very image of God's substance. He upholds all things by the word of His power. He is superior to the angels in name and nature, for He made them. After purging our sins He was enthroned on high at the right hand of God in heaven.

1. There can be no higher means of Divine communication than by the Son. Others have been inspired, but He is the Truth itself. The Word of God does not need to come to Him Who is the Word. All true inspiration, viz. of the Holy Spirit, invariably points to Christ.

The author wrote not long ago a brief discussion on "Inspiration Explains Itself." After it was published he realized with chagrin that he had left out half the subject, namely, that inspiration is as much needed to read as to write the Word of God. God the Holy Spirit is as essential to our getting the message from Him as He is to the giving of it. If we know not how to pray as we ought without the help of the Holy Spirit, neither are we able to receive God's Word as we ought or speak it faithfully and effectually except by the same inspiration of the Holy Spirit.

While Christ is God speaking to us, the Holy Spirit dwells in Him without measure; and only by the same Holy Spirit can we know Christ, see Him as He is, trust Him as He deserves. It is in the Christ that the Holy Spirit is most untrammelled in complete utterance of Himself. By His Incarnation the Son is God made visible and understandable to faith and to following. Never was flesh so Divinely eloquent as when "the Word was made flesh." And never does the heart of man speak so freely and effectually of Redemption in Christ as when the Holy Spirit in that heart is the real Author of the utterance.

2. In the mystery of His Person the Incarnate Son is the solution of the problem and enigma of sin. Here one mystery serves to solve another, and by the mystery of His Person we can master this mystery of iniquity. There is a degree in which the Person of Christ apart from Redemption from sin tends to be incomprehensible. He is the Divine answer also to the otherwise inpenetrable problem of sin. Using the foolish figure of men, one might say of the crucifixion—God turned the Trinity inside out to end the utter darkness in iniquity. Into that midnight blackness shone the internal glory of the triunity[10] of the Godhead. Redemption from sin was the occasion of God's greatest manifestation of Himself to us in glorious triumph of Redeeming love.

3. We were not here to see Christ in His great work of creation; but we are here to see Him in His greater work of re-creation. Without the latter, creation, because of sin following it, would have been shrouded in dense darkness. Christ put Himself into re-creation as He could not into creation alone, for in Redemption the Creator dedicated Himself to re-creation.

The writer of Hebrews resembles John in setting forth the preëxistence and unqualified Deity of the Son. Like John he links our destiny in glory to that of the Christ. I John 3:2 says, "Beloved, now are we the children of God, and it is not yet made manifest

[10] In the Trinity there are four unities, three within the Three Persons, and the fourth within the Trinity itself. Unless each Person was a unity, there could not be the perfect, transcendent unity of the Godhead Itself.

what we shall be. We know that if He (or it) shall be manifested, we shall be like Him; for we shall see Him as He is." Hebrews 10: 12-14 says, "He when He had offered one sacrifice for ever, sat down on the right hand of God. . . . For by one offering hath He perfected (consummated) for ever them that are sanctified."

4. Blessed be God! We are on our way to this consummation through Him who is the Way; and we possess the truth of Him who is the Truth. Further, we live evermore by the Life of Him who is the life of all who live indeed. Though as yet our sonship is little more than the echo of that in the Son Himself, nevertheless it is grounded in what He is to us and to the Father. Rejoicing in the capacity for God which He put in us by creation, we rejoice still more that by re-creation He fills that capacity in us with Himself as the unfailing means of ultimately becoming perfected sons. Then, to the Redeemer-Creator, to save man was more important than to call into being and shape into symmetry the whole material universe. In ourselves we cannot find thought or word to tell why this Saviour loves us so, because the reason of grace is not in us but in Him.

5. This Divine-human Person is the final form and supreme substance of God's greatest manifestation of Himself in Self-sacrifice, Self-impartation, and Self-fulfilment. This implies that the sovereignty of the Father runs right through the process of that fulfilment of the Divine purpose, plan and nature. From our

situation on this sin-cursed earth we see all too prominently ugly, hideous, ungodly sin still crucifying Christ afresh in its treatment of His followers. Iniquity tortured Him to the last heart-beat as it broke, never to beat again even in His risen body, for in Him a new and everlasting means of life replaced that of blood and heart-beats. Looking up to the Throne of Divine Sovereignty, we may see supreme over all earthly movements the unfailing purposes of the Father running through the centuries heading for the final manifestation in Judgment where every knee shall bend before the Son, and every tongue confess His absolute supremacy.

6. Nowhere in all the Scriptures is the Person of Christ set forth in higher terms or in stronger measures than in this Epistle. It shows the existence and life of the Father as inseparable from those of the Son. The God and Father, the Saviour and Sanctifier are more glorious in manifestation and holy in substance than can be seen except by the great light of the Holy Spirit's illumination. The ministry of our Lord required the inclusion of our nature in His Person. He took up as Prophet, Priest, and King or Revealer, Redeemer and Ruler the offices necessary to making us kings and priests unto God that we might be filled with all the fulness of Him that filleth all in all, for of His fulness have we all received. This Epistle begins in chapter 3:1 the outline of the office of the Son in the Redemption of Man: "Wherefore, holy brethren, partakers of the heavenly calling, consider the Apostle and High Priest of our confession, even Jesus."

II. The Priesthood of Christ

The fulness and sufficiency of the Priesthood of our Lord as set forth in the Epistle to the Hebrews has a message for the Christian Church of unsurpassable importance. Had its teaching been heeded through the centuries, the unity of the Church, its spirituality, and its power to evangelize the world would have been sustained. An order of priesthood in the Church has arisen which is not only superfluous and spurious, but also immeasurably injurious. It is both unspiritual and devitalizing to give time and strength to that rendered utterly obsolete by the fulness and perfect sufficiency of the Priesthood of Christ when by Him all by faith can have access to God.

1. Many members and denominations of the Christian Church have most positive aversion to this anomalous priesthood prevalent in some communions. The Roman, the Greek Catholic and several others have an ecclesiastical priesthood not at all in keeping with New Testament Christianity. The substitution of this order of priestly practice is the largest single factor within the Church in seriously damaging its integrity and retarding its progress. Plainly, the bondage to this perverse priesthood is in direct contradiction to the completeness of Christ's own Priesthood, and obscures the blood-bought privilege, namely, that every follower of Christ has through Him immediate access to God in Redemption without the superfluous ministry of ecclesiastical priests and potentates. Nowhere in the Bible is there clearer teaching on what should be the

Christ-intended character of the ministry in the Christian Church than in this Epistle before us.

2. The Priesthood of the Jewish faith was appointed of God and was therefore legitimate in its day. It served to prepare the way for the coming of the King High Priest. The priest and the high priests of the Old Covenant have passed out of the picture, because the New Covenant has annulled all that. The smoking altars and the sprinkling of the blood of beasts have passed away because the Great Sacrifice and the Great High Priest in the immediate presence of God has rendered forever obsolete the whole Hebrew economy of the Levitical Priesthood and practice. This does not mean that we are to despise the old order of priests and sacrifices. But it does mean that to revert to it after the New Covenant with God has been established is worse than useless, even atavistic. Official human nature is always very slow to give up its place of special privilege. Its self-importance would rather magnify its office, no matter how much that office had been outgrown. Whether official or not, human nature is seldom as ready to seek divine help as to look for mere human assistance. The history of the Hebrew people shows similar repeated folly in preferring pagan alliance to Jehovah's help.

3. The manifest purpose of the writer of this Epistle to save Hebrew Christians from backsliding into the hole of the pit from which they had been dug, is similar to that of Paul in Galatians and elsewhere. While the Temple ceremonies remained, there would

be strong inclination to turn back to the observance of the Levitical priests.

4. In all religions, pagan included, the office of the priest was that of a man regarded as holy because he ministered before God or the gods for those who wished him so to do. Because of Jehovah's majesty and holiness the people feared to come before Him. "For they could not endure that which was enjoined. If even a beast touch the mountain, it shall be stoned; and so fearful was the appearance, that Moses said, I exceedingly fear and quake" (12:20, 21).

The priest was required to offer gifts and sacrifices to God for the people. Because appointed of God he was allowed to do this. But into the Holy of Holies only the high priest entered once a year. In general, the blessing and favor of God was not sought by the people personally, but through the appointed ministry of the priests. The people's sense of sin incapacitated them from coming unto God for themselves.

5. The method which this writer of the Epistle followed was to alternate teaching, as already said, with exhortation. He shows himself a master of strong yet tactful admonition. He defines well. For example, as to the angels he says, "Are they not all ministering spirits, sent forth to do service for the sake of them that shall inherit salvation?"

6. The first mention of Christ as High Priest occurs in 2:17; "Wherefore it behooved Him in all things to be made like unto His brethren, that He might become a merciful and faithful high priest in things pertaining

to God, to make propitiation for the sins of the people." Here the plan is to discuss in the main the *Character of Christ's High Priesthood.* We have already discussed the nature of propitiation as the power to blot sin out of existence, completely to exterminate it. The meaning of expiate, as some give in place of propitiate, should be discussed under the head of the nature of Christ's Sacrifice. The passage quoted deals with the character of Christ's priesthood in mercy and faithfulness because of His perfect humanity.

In 3:1, the next place where the expression is used, "the Apostle and High Priest of our confession," there is the addition in the word "Apostle" which evidently refers to His Priesthood as *delegated.* He was the "Sent One," the Divine Messenger Priest. But He was that Message as well as the Messenger. The "heavenly calling" refers no doubt to the High Priest of the New Covenant as Divinely appointed. When Jesus calls us "brethren," it means that we have a brother on the throne of the universe, for He is the King High Priest.[11] That is the richest relative a poor sinner ever has, for "we are joint heirs with Christ." "Our fellowship is with the Father and with the Son, Jesus Christ." "He hath been counted worthy of more glory than Moses, by so much as he that built the house hath more honor than the house. . . . But He that built all things is God. . . . But Christ as a Son, over His house; whose house we are." . . . Hence He is the Builder, King, High Priest and Messenger of the Mercy of God, and that Mercy itself. As to the two founders of the two Coven-

[11] The enthronement is expressed more fully at the close of Revelation—"The throne of God and of the Lamb."

ants, no fault is found with Moses that the Old Covenant could do so little, for "the Law made nothing perfect"; and Christ did not come to destroy the Law, but to fulfil it.

7. Following on through the successive mentions of Christ as High Priest we come next to 4: 14-16, "Having then a great high priest, who hath passed through the heavens, Jesus the Son of God, let us hold fast our confession. For we have not an high priest that cannot be touched with the feeling of our infirmities; but one that hath been in all points tempted like as we are, yet without sin." Even so Jesus passed through the created heavens into the uncreated heaven of the immediate presence of God. This indicates the accepted merit of His death, and the divine institution of His faithful function as great High Priest. There His wholly sanctified humanity serves in heaven for us. The high priests of the law were beset with infirmity for which the law provided sacrifices for sins of ignorance and inadvertence. Our High Priest, while as sympathetic in His Deity as in His humanity, was also sensitive to human susceptibility to sin and yet He was without sin. So we are bidden hold fast our confession of His effectual sympathy with our infirmity of body, soul and spirit. While "Mortal spirits tire and faint," the integrity of His priesthood on our behalf remains to encourage boldness in coming unto the throne of grace, "that we may receive mercy, and may find grace to help us in time of need."

8. In the next paragraph, 5: 1-10, there is presented a comparison of the priests of the First Covenant with

the High Priest of the New Covenant. Taken from among men, the former were appointed to offer unto God gifts and sacrifices. They had a fellow-feeling for those to whom they ministered, for like them they were compassed with infirmity. None of these priests, however, were self-appointed, but had the honor of being called of God as was Aaron.

> "So Christ also glorified not Himself to be made a high priest, but He that spake unto Him, Thou art my Son, This day have I begotten Thee: as He saith also in another place, Thou art a priest for ever after the order of Melchizedek."

Because our Lord did not need to offer up sacrifice for Himself, He could offer up Himself as a sacrifice for us all. And because He did not need to be forgiven, He could minister forgiveness to all who call upon Him. Though He was sinless He was not prayerless, especially on that Passover night before His death.

> "Who in the days of His flesh, having offered up prayers and supplications with strong crying and tears unto Him that was able to save Him from death (rather, out of, *ek*, death), and having been heard for His godly fear, though He was a Son, yet learned obedience (realized it) by the things which He suffered; and having been perfected, He became unto all them that obey Him the author (cause) of eternal salvation; named of God a high priest after the order of Melchizedek."

From John 10:18 we learn that the Father had commanded Him to submit to this suffering. But He did not naturally or supernaturally desire this suffering and death. If He had desired to be crucified by sin and thus tortured to death by it, He would have been abnormal, unnatural, eccentric, morbid, disordered, deranged, fanatic, or infatuated like some of the early Christians who determinedly sought martyrdom.

Here again we have the expression "having been made perfect." This does not imply previous imperfection in wrong, evil, or sin; but perfected as the bud is in the flower. Our Lord grew in wisdom and in stature. There was a continued process of personal growth we call self-realization. This is perfected when complete in consummation of the Father's purpose or the fulfilment of His will in sacrificial attainment.

9. Among the outstanding characteristics of the priesthood of Christ, the order of Melchizedek is important. There was but one Melchizedek, so far as the Old Testament record goes. He belonged to that priesthood in no lineal way. Archeology has corroborated the fact of his existence. He did not inherit the office, nor did he have a son as his successor in it. It came to him by moral and personal outstanding excellence. He combined the offices of king and of priest. As king of Salem he was king of peace, and his name signifies in Hebrew that he was also king of righteousness. It was accounted that he was superior to Abraham, having received tithes from him. This gives Melchizedek as priest precedence over the whole Aaronic order of priesthood. In the third century a sect arose which paid him divine honors as superior to Christ Himself.

10. In 7:11 ff it is argued that Christ's priesthood because He descended from Judah and not from Levi, was not "after the law of a carnal commandment, but after the power of an endless life" (Greek, an indissoluble life). It is more than passing strange that in the providence of God this Melchizedek with the pure

monotheistic faith should be raised up before Israel, and of a type of priesthood far superior to that of the Aaronic. How much more marvelous that the priesthood of Christ should be in heaven as the highest ideal even for there, even as Melchizedek was the highest ideal on earth. Neither of them were formally set apart to the priesthood. Both remain the ideal forever because of the character each had in personal superiority. It is an order of priesthood that in the nature of the case is immortal. That which it does is accepted of God and abides ever in Him. It was for Christ to be High Priest and have an eternal priesthood in the presence of God. The Levitical priesthood passes away and is fulfilled in that of the King - High Priesthood of Christ. The Covenants share the fate of their representative priesthood. The Old Covenant has passed away. The New Covenant will abide forever. The law proved men's guilt, but could take it away only provisionally, depending on the coming sacrifice in Christ. The New Covenant has nothing provisional and temporary. It ministers "eternal salvation." Its priesthood assures unsullied righteousness and perfect peace. "By so much also hath Jesus become the surety of a better covenant." This by the law of the greatness of His Personality.

11. The permanent and perfect character of Christ's priesthood arises from being God-made. Chapter 7:17 says, "Thou art a priest for ever after the order of Melchizedek." The priestly ministries on earth must pass away because neither perfect nor intended to be

permanent, for they were on earth amidst things passing away. But Christ's ministry is in heaven. Of all ministries His is the highest and best; and appropriately is rendered in the true tabernacle built by God, not by man. And this means that His ministry abides for ever in that heavenly tabernacle which can never be superseded, for there "He ever liveth to make intercession for us." So He serves in heaven for us forever, for as we next learn, His priesthood is unchangeable.

In 7: 21-25, "But He (has been made a priest) with an oath by (or through) Him that saith of (or unto) Him, the Lord sware and will not repent Himself, Thou art a priest for ever; by so much also hath Jesus become the surety of a better covenant. But He because He abideth for ever, hath a priesthood unchangeable (Inviolable)." Here again we have mention of the better nature of the New Covenant, better in its law (not external), in its knowledge of God, better in brotherhood, better with new nature in human personality, and a better tabernacle of one vast chamber, instead of the three small divisions as in the tabernacle on earth. Moreover, that Old Covenant was a *system* that in the New has been replaced by a *Person.* All systems on earth tend to become soul-less; but the Mediator-Person of the New Covenant could change only for the worse, because He cannot change for any better, for better there cannot be. And His Priesthood is divinely pledged to the unchangeable in character and permanence by the very oath of the Most High God.

12. Next, in 8: 1, 2, we read, "Now in the things

which we are saying, the chief point is this: we have such a high priest, who sat down on the right hand of the throne of the Majesty in the heavens, a minister of the sanctuary and of the true tabernacle, which the Lord pitched and not man." We note He is seated and not standing as were all earthly priests, for He is King as well as High Priest. He is seated in permanence, agreeing with what has already been said. His is a throne which can never be shaken or pass to another. He sits in the highest place of Divine honor, on the right hand of God the Father. In the true Tabernacle the Better High Priest enters with the true offering and is received and enthroned by and with the Father who shares His eternal throne with Him.

Finally on this matter, chapter 8:6 says, "But now hath He obtained a ministry the more excellent, by so much as He is also the mediator of a better covenant, which hath been enacted on better promises." This is not a climax preparing for a descent, but an infinite attainment that will be maintained forever. As He is the only Godman, He is the only Mediator, for there is One Mediator between God and man, the man Christ Jesus. In Him is the better promise in every way surpassing all others, the promise of life eternal that will take all eternity to interpret and exhaust its fulness of meaning.

The roots of the wondrous tree of Christ's High Priesthood are in proportion to the Tree of Life itself. His everlasting priesthood is rooted in His eternal Sonship. Men on earth were elevated to the priesthood, but Christ elevated the Priesthood itself to infinity of power, merit, value and glory.

The story of the enthronement of the Christ of Sacrifice comes out in fullest measure in the apocalyptic unfolding of the Book of Revelation. Suffer a few among its many statements of this.

In Rev. 5:12—

"Worthy is the Lamb that hath been slain to receive the power, and riches, and wisdom, and might, and honour, and glory, and blessing."

In Rev. 11:15—

"The kingdom of the world is become that of our Lord, and of His Christ: and He shall reign for ever and ever."

In Rev. 22: 1, 3—

"And he showed me a river of water of life, bright as crystal, proceeding out of the throne of God and of the Lamb . . . And there shall be no curse any more: and the throne of God and of the Lamb shall be there."

Chapter Five

THE VITAL IN CHRIST'S SACRIFICE

Introduction

Jesus Christ is the most thought-about Person in human history. What a Babel of estimates, interpretations and evaluations have been offered to explain Him! "What think ye of Christ?" is the old question that will not down. "Whose son is He?" The Scriptures say, the Son of God and the son of Mary. Is not He "the seed of the woman" sent to bruise the serpent's head?

The word "son" is a great term of classification in rank or likeness. For example, "the sons of Belial" were like the Evil One in worthlessness. "Sons of Elohim" were the mighty ones. "Sons of Thunder," the loud, noisy ones. The term "son" means more than similarity. Usually it points to personal relation in education or generation. The "Sons of the Prophets" were their disciples. For Christ to be called "The Son of God" meant that He was classed with God.

1. In the Patristic Period and as late as the time of Athanasius the relation of the Divine Son to the Father

was thought to be by "Eternal Generation."[12] This if subjective becoming is but eternal impossibility. No one can be eternally coming into existence. That would not fitly present Christ the Eternal Son in preëxistence. Surely the Preëxistent Son was the Eternal Logos whom God the Father forever needed in manifesting Himself. As transcendent the Father had ever found indispensable the Eternal Son to represent Him, to act for Him in all relation, or else be forever buried in His transcendence, even as the Holy Spirit was ever needed for all Divine impartation to the end of fellowship in fulfilment of the Father's sovereignty.

2. That Christianity, the religion of Redemption unto unity in God, should break into so many denominational divisions, is certainly remarkably strange. And equally strange is it that the Great Sacrifice of God in Christ to destroy sin's disunity, should have almost as many interpretations of its meaning as there are denominations. In this presentation we take it that the blood of Christ was His sacrificial life poured out in death that thereby He might be enabled to give Himself in ever-living self-impartation that alone could exterminate sin.

Peter, when walking on the boisterous waves, took his eyes off the Master. At once he began to sink. So do any of our interpretations of Redemption when we no longer see Jesus and Him only. John 12:26 tells us that certain Greeks said to Philip, "Sir, we would see Jesus." Would that all theorists on this subject

[12] However, it is but fair to say that the idea of eternal generation was instrumental rather than objective. The Son was the eternal Power or Person of generating or creating.

had the same intent. Infallibly, however, we project our interpreting content of mind into whatever we see or consider. As this content of mind endlessly differs in various minds, what we see in Christ or His death equally differs. Unless we have the similar re-creation of personality in the image of Christ, and our minds become filled with the Word's appreciation of Him, we cannot come to unity of thought about Him. A great appreciation brought to pass by the same causes, naturally leads toward unity of thinking. When persons are aflame with burning devotion to Christ because of what He is to them and has done for them, then the great central Mind of God in Christ is reproduced and may fill all such individual minds with its own vital vision.

I. The Mediator of the New Covenant

There is a most important and intimate relation between the Personal Word and the Written Word of God. What a tangle of impossible puzzle the Scriptures would be without Christ; and how very much less would we know of Him without the precious pages of both the Old and the New Testaments! We have been learning from this Epistle to the Hebrews the colorful and consistent character of our Lord's Priesthood. We come now to the sacrifice of Christ in preparation for its mediation. We have noted that in the fulness of His ministry He is both High Priest and also the incomparable Sacrifice which He offered.

1. How different was that which was happening at the same time on earth and in heaven. On earth He

was suffering as the victim of merciless human sin without the gates of the city. Dying, He entered the Heavenly Holy of Holies to become the perpetual ever-living sacrifice there unto God for us. His entry there was to share the throne with the Father, for He was seated at His Right Hand, the highest place of acceptance and honor. There "He ever liveth to make intercession for us." As King - High Priest He is at the same time the accepted perpetual Personal Presence before the Father. This is "the throne of God and of the Lamb."

2. There are at least four ways in which the offering of Christ as High Priest was made in acceptance and thereby in efficacy. The most frequent way mentioned is that in the Blood. Some passages like 9:14, which we discuss later on in this chapter, have double result expressed. "How much more shall the blood of Christ, who through eternal Spirit offered Himself without blemish unto God, cleanse your conscience from dead works to serve the living God." There are really three mentioned in this passage, Blood, Spirit and Himself. Evidently it means when He gave His blood, He gave Himself, His life, and this through the eternal sacrificial Spirit of God. In the eighteenth verse of the same chapter: "Wherefore even the first covenant hath not been dedicated without blood." The inference is that the blood of Christ was that with which the New Covenant was *sealed* or *dedicated.*[13] The further explanation

[13] Three ministries of the Blood are mentioned—The sealing of the New Covenant; the transfusion in giving Christ's life to the New Nature; and the cleansing from sin from the beginning to the end of the Christian life.

is offered that "*According to the law* (of the old covenant) . . . apart from the shedding of blood there is no remission (forgiveness)." Chapter 10:19, "Having therefore, brethren, boldness to enter into the holy place by the blood of Jesus, by the way which He dedicated for us, a new and living way, through the veil, that is to say His flesh, and (having) a great priest over the house of God . . ." Here, though the blood speaks of death, it is called "a new and living way," for if Christ had but died and not risen, it would not have been a new and living way. Chapter 13:12, "Wherefore Jesus also, that He might sanctify the people through His own blood, suffered without the gate," where the original sanctuary was situated.

Other passages from other scriptures are: Eph. 1:7, "In whom we have our redemption through His blood." Col. 1:20, "Having made peace through the blood of His cross." I Cor. 11:25, "This cup is the New Covenant in my blood." Rev. 5: 6, 9: "A Lamb standing as though it had been slain . . . for thou wast slain, and didst purchase unto God with thy blood (men) of every tribe, and tongue, and people, and nation, and madest them to be unto our God a kingdom and priests." Rev. 7:14, "And they washed their robes and made them white in the blood of the Lamb." Rev. 12:11, "And they overcame him (the devil) because of the blood of the Lamb, and because of the word of their testimony."

3. A number of passages speak of *the sacrifice of Christ in person.* We have already noted (Heb. 9:14),

"Offered Himself without blemish unto God." Also in the twenty-fifth verse: "Wherefore He is able to save to the uttermost them that draw near unto God through Him, seeing He ever liveth to make intercession for them." Again in 7:27, "For this He did once for all, when He offered up Himself." Also in 9:28, "So Christ also, having been once offered to bear the sins of many."

4. There is, moreover, the mention of *the offering of Christ's body*. Heb. 10:10, "By which will we have been sanctified through the offering of the body of Christ once for all." Peter also speaks of Christ's bearing away our sins in His own body on the tree. In the same chapter, twelfth verse, the means or way is simply by *Sacrifice*: "But He, when He had offered one sacrifice for sins forever, sat down on the right hand of God." Doubtless this is the sacrifice of Himself, body included.

5. God instituted the Covenant of the Law with Moses as its mediator, while he lived. God also instituted the New Covenant with Christ as its Mediator in an endless life. This means, of course, that the benefits of this Better Covenant are ministered or transmitted to us by Him in His self-impartation to us after re-creation of us, and especially by the Holy Spirit's inhabitation.

Remembering that this new Covenant is like that with Abraham, an unconditional promise, will, testament, or bequeathment, it is His blessed office to put into our very persons as well as into our possession what it has for us. He is the Living Media or Mediator by which that He has for us, is passed on to us. This New Covenant without a living Mediator would be a will without an executor. This Divine Redemption is something which cannot be obtained apart from the Divine Redeemer; for it was instituted in our favor by His death as the Divine Will. It is made effective by the ministry of His Redeeming Life. This Greatest Bequeathment or Will that ever has been, or can be made, was established, that is, came into force when He died. Its infinite and eternal benefits are imparted by the vital contact of His Redemptive Person in everlasting perpetuity.

6. First in 7:22 it is said that "Jesus hath become the surety of a better covenant," and in 9:15, "He is the mediator of a new testament." So He is both Mediator and Surety of this New Covenant. This means that He is Sponsor to see that its provisions are carried out. So He is the surety that this will or testament in our favor becomes effective. It was established on better, that is unconditional promises. So to speak, the Mediator goes security for the testament or will being made good. It is Christ to whom we look for the fulfilling of this bequeathment. As to wills, a faithful executor is all-important. And the greater the bequeathment, the more important the faithfulness of the Mediator. It is as if one bequeathed us a vast fortune, made the will effective by his death; and then rose from the dead to be its executor. This is exactly what our Lord Jesus Christ has done on our behalf. He is Mediator in two directions. First, before the Father to settle the

account for our sins. Having done this by offering Himself for us through death, He appears the ever-living sacrifice before the Father to make us heirs and joint-heirs with Him. There His will in our favor is recorded in the New Testament, the New Covenant bequeathment. And He being Mediator of this New Testament or Covenant, is Mediator in our direction, to dispense the blessing and the benefits of His will on our behalf.

II. The Sacrifice and Service of Christ's Blood

In Philippians 2:17, "Yea, and if I am offered upon the sacrifice and service of your faith, I joy and rejoice with you all." How like this Disciple and Apostle to his Master. In this Epistle, Hebrews 12:2, "Looking unto Jesus the author and perfecter (architect and contractor) of our faith, who for the joy that was set before Him endured the cross, despising shame, and hath sat down at the right hand of the throne of God."

The sacrifices of the First Covenant were sacrifices in faith, faith that wrought obedience. Those who offered them were told, yea, commanded what to do. The sinless blood of unwitting animals was poured out. No body was taken into the holy of holies. Only the blood of the innocent sacrificed victims was taken in there and sprinkled by the high priest according to directions. No high priest entered with his own blood as an offering. That would be no good whether shed or unshed.

1. Christ did not enter the Holy of Holies *with* the blood of another, but *by* His own blood, having poured

out His life unto death. And He passed into the absolutely immediate presence of God. No doubt, though the writer does not mention it here, His possible second entering was because of His resurrection following His death and the shedding of His blood, and His ascension following His resurrection after forty days. His offering of not only His crucified and risen body, but of Himself (both are mentioned), enabled Him to enter where no priest on earth could come. There is the question whether this entering was before or after His ascension. As there may have been two enterings, the first would be without His body, the second with His risen body. The first entering would then be in keeping with the new covenant in the first phase; the second, by the new covenant in the second phase. In the first He came as Mediator for all mankind, having by the sacrifice of Himself put away their sins once for all: in the second He came to take up His Mediatorship of impartation and bequeathment. *At death* and, of course, without His body He committed Himself into the loving hands and arms of the Father, having finished His redeeming obedience and suffering. In the second, not only had the death of His body been undone, but it had been made serviceable to His great work of sacrifice in imparting or outpouring His eternal life through its open wounds, to all persons turning to Him as Saviour.

2. Chapter 9:11 ff, "But Christ having come a high priest of the good things to come, through the greater and more perfect tabernacle, not made with hands, that

is to say, not of this creation, nor yet through the blood of goats and calves, but through His own blood, entered in once for all into the holy place, having obtained eternal redemption. . . . How much more shall the blood of Christ who through eternal spirit offered Himself without blemish unto God." (See earlier discussion of this matter.)

As we say in the last chapter, III, 4, the Revised Version gives us alternate readings, "*the* eternal Spirit," or "*His* eternal Spirit." As a matter of fact neither is correct. Neither is in the original Greek. There is the eternal Holy Spirit; but this is evidently not meant. All three Persons of the Holy Trinity are intrinsically, foundationally, and eternally sacrificial in spirit. Therefore it is spirit not peculiar to the Son alone, but is *the spirit of the entire Godhead.* The spirit of the Father and of the Holy Spirit was in the Son; and by this spirit in common in the Holy Trinity the Son offered Himself without blemish unto God. Surely this has vastly richer meaning and implications.

III. The Sacrifice of Christ

All Three Persons of the Trinity are infinitely sacrificial in inter-relation to each other; but the Son is the full personalization of Sacrifice for sin. In a way the very Universe also is sacrificial, because none of it exists for its own sake. When man was made in the image of God, he was created a sacrificial being; but sin turned him into the disunity of selfishness within, and toward God, and also in relation to fellow-man. But God then required sacrifices from sinners, and from

Abel on they were offered in worship or for sin. The offering for iniquity required three things: it must be specified by God and not chosen by the one who offered it; it must be perfect or unblemished; and it must be presented to God in the way which He appointed. We find that the whole system of Old Testament offerings had their deepest meaning, value and virtue in being fore-gleams of the coming Great Sacrifice in Christ.

1. In the Old Covenant there were the gift-sacrifices and those for sin. In the New Covenant there was the Redeeming sacrifice of Christ in Person by His death. And there were the sacrifices of the Christian life in response to the infinite sacrifice by and in our Lord. For example, in the close of this Epistle, 12:16, we read, "But to do good and to communicate forget not: for with such sacrifices God is well pleased." This reminds us of what Paul in Phil. 4:8 terms, "a sacrifice acceptable, well-pleasing to God," referring to the church gifts sent to him. In Eph. 5:3 he refers to the sacrifice of Redemption: "Even as Christ also loved you, and gave Himself up for us, an offering and a sacrifice unto God." A perpetual Priesthood requires a perpetual Offering, the ever-living Son, crucified and risen from the dead. The Incarnation was a sacrifice of God, and also there was the personal sacrifice of the Son during His earthly life. Every act in all His incarnate days expressed that He Himself was a sacrifice unto God for sinners. The emphasis on this sacrifice in Person by death as in life runs through all this Epistle to the Hebrews. But there is His vital, personal sacri-

fice for us after His death—His Living Sacrifice. In chapter 7:27 we read, "For such a high priest became us, holy, guileless, undefiled, separate from sinners, *and made higher than the heavens. . . .* For this He did once for all, when He offered up Himself." This sacrificial death needed no repetition. His sacrificial life after death is to be eternal. That also emphasizes the voluntary character of His death. No compulsion! No blaming His murderers! No break with the Father because of penalty-passion taking it out on Him! Not a scintilla or shadow of spiritual death! How could a high priest, higher than the heavens, offering up Himself unto God for sin, die spiritually in that holy act of obedience unto God and for man? That death which did not break fellowship with the Father was a long, long step to further their eternal fellowship.

2. It would seem that the Holy Spirit had in foreview the false theory called "Eternal Atonement," namely, that God had in the infinite ages before the world was, suffered in anticipation of sin, and ever since has suffered because of it, and will in all the eternity to come continue to suffer in remembrance of it, and that Christ's sufferings were but a show-window sample of the Divine, for He did not so much make atonement as reveal "the eternal atonement." (I am here as indicated using the terms of this theory). We may note that this Epistle does not give the slightest support anyhow or anywhere to that Christ-robbing interpretation. Here is the inspired reply to it: Chapter 9:24 ff., "Christ entered into heaven itself, now to appear before the face of God for us: nor yet that

He should offer Himself often . . . else must He often have suffered since the foundation of the world; but now once at the end of the ages hath He been manifested to put away sin by the sacrifice of Himself." Spiritus Sanctus dixit.

3. In this Epistle (9: 14) there is a repetition about our Lord offering up Himself: "Christ, Who through eternal spirit offered Himself without blemish unto God." This is repeated in verse 27, "So Christ also, having been once offered to bear the sins of many." In 10:10 we have the form of expression somewhat varied: "By which will (of God) we have been sanctified through the offering of the body of Jesus Christ once for all." What precedes this statement, explains it. Speaking of the better sacrifice of the New Covenant, mention is made of the Incarnation body, prophesied about and prepared for the Son. He came to fulfil the Father's will in surrendering it to sacrifice in death. So on the third day He was perfected, and the Divine will consummated. This passage in Heb. 10:10 reminds us of I Peter 2: 24, "Who His own self bare (carried up) our sins in His body upon the tree." The discussion goes on to say in verses 12 and 14, "But He when He had offered one sacrifice for sins for ever, sat down on the right hand of God. . . . For by one offering hath He perfected (consummated) for ever them that are sanctified." The Eternal Atonement Theory itself, according to these scriptures, appears in need of being atoned for.

IV. The Lamb of God

That we may consider further the Redeeming Sacrifice of Christ as set forth in other scriptures, we must break away from the Epistle to the Hebrews. With only three exceptions the sacred expression, "the Lamb of God," is confined to the Revelation. I Peter 1:18, 19 says, "Knowing that ye were redeemed, not with corruptible things . . . but with precious blood, as of a lamb without blemish and without spot, even the blood of Christ." This must be taken as a clear statement that the blood of the Lamb of God is included with the Son Himself in the mighty means of Redemption.

The beloved disciple John says that John the Baptist twice used this expression named: John 1:29, 36, "Behold the Lamb of God that taketh (or beareth, *airōn*) away the sin of the world." This was said to those gathered where he was baptizing. The day previous he had answered a deputation from the priests and Levites inquiring who he (John) professed himself to be. He denied that he was the Messiah. It was on the day following this that John saw Jesus approaching. Being filled with the Holy Spirit from his mother's womb, John was fitly endowed to discern and designate Jesus as he did. On the next day after this, to two of his disciples John repeats the confession, "Behold the Lamb of God." Inspired by the Holy Spirit, John thus prophetically and most aptly described the Christ of God as the Divinely appointed Sacrifice for the sin of the world.

1. Turning now to the Revelation, we find in 1:2

that the Lord Himself is the real author of this Book, and that John is serving as His amanuensis. Some twenty-eight times this remarkable expression, "the Lamb," occurs and is applied to the Christ after His death and enthronement. This shows that Christ considered the Divine Redemptive Sacrifice as perpetuated in Himself. This is not only plainly apparent, but all important in establishing that its substance is *Personal.* It agrees perfectly with the Scriptures that Christ offered, not His death alone, but Himself by means of His death. "He is the propitiation for our sins." *He is our Redemption,* "the redemption that is in Christ Jesus" (Rom. 3:24).

2. The first instance is in 5:6, "I saw in the midst of the throne . . . a Lamb standing as though it had been slain." Here we have the announcement of the enthronement, not merely of Divine Sacrifice, but also of the One who made it, for the figure of "the Lamb" combines both meanings. This makes known that the Father is sharing forever with the Son His throne in the reign of Redemption. In two verses later, all persons about the throne are prostrating themselves before the Lamb; and in verse 12 we hear the acclaim of the vast numbers, "Ten thousand times ten thousand, and thousands of thousands saying with a great voice, Worthy is the Lamb that hath been slain to receive the power, and riches, and wisdom, and might, and honor, and glory, and blessing." These are joined in this anthem of praise by throngs throughout the universe: "Unto Him that sitteth on the throne, and unto the Lamb, be the blessing, and the honor, and the glory,

and the dominion, for ever and ever" (or unto the ages of the ages). This is quite a reversal from what happened on earth when Christ became the Lamb of God's sacrifice for sin.

3. In 6:1 we find the Lamb opening one of the seven seals of prophecy; and in verse 16 the unspeakable fear of the unsaved and their calling to rocks and mountains to fall on them and hide them in the caves from "the face of Him that sitteth on the throne, and from the wrath of the Lamb: for the great day of their wrath is come; and who is able to stand?" Here really the figure of the sacrificial Lamb is transcended, and to Him is attributed the wrath of righteous indignation.

In 7:9, 10 the reverse comes when the vast numbers of the saved from all nations are "standing before the Lamb, arrayed in white robes, and palms in their hands; and they cry with a great voice, saying, Salvation unto our God who sitteth on the throne and unto the Lamb." Verse 14, "These are they that come out of the great tribulation, and they washed their robes, and they made them white in the blood of the Lamb. . . . For the Lamb that is in the midst of the throne shall be their shepherd, and shall guide them unto fountains of waters of life: and God shall wipe away every tear from their eyes." So the Lamb of God becomes the Good Shepherd.

In 12:11 the scene changes to the triumph over the great accuser of the saints day and night: "And they overcame him because of the blood of the Lamb, and because of the word of their testimony; and they loved not their life even unto death." That is not unlike this very day.

In 13:8 we have the much needed correction of the mistranslation, "the Lamb slain from the foundation of the world." That would be a long time for Him to be lying dead. The passage should read: "And all that dwell on the earth shall worship Him, every one whose name hath not been written from the foundation of the world in the book of life of the Lamb that hath been slain." This translation is strikingly corroborated by 17:8, "They whose name hath not been written in the book of life from the foundation of the world."

4. In 14:1, "And I saw, and behold the Lamb standing on the Mount Zion." Verse 4, "Those are they that follow the Lamb whithersoever He goeth. These were purchased from among men to be the firstfruits unto God and unto the Lamb. And in their mouth was found no lie: they are without blemish." They were keeping company with Him who is the Truth. Chapter 15:3, "And they sing the song of Moses the servant of God, and the song of the Lamb." Chapter 17:14, "These enemies shall war against the Lamb, and the Lamb shall overcome them, for He is Lord of lords, and King of kings." Let pacifists note, in these days of war plagues, the sky overhung with war clouds, it is well to know that even the Lamb finds it necessary to go to war, though He is the Prince of peace. The nineteenth chapter is one of triumphs and praises. In verses seven and nine there is the wedding announcement of the Lamb's marriage to the Church Bride; and "blessed

are they that are bidden to the marriage supper of the Lamb." In 21:23 the City of God is pictured. "And I saw no temple (sanctuary) therein; for the Lord God the Almighty and the Lamb are the temple (sanctuary) thereof. And the city hath no need of the sun, neither of the moon, to shine upon it; for the glory of God did light it, and the lamp thereof is the Lamb." "But only they written in the Lamb's book of life" are to be its citizens. In 22:1 and 3 we have the conclusion. From out the throne of God and of the Lamb flows the river of the water of life, clear as crystal. "And there shall be no curse any more; and the throne of God and of the Lamb shall be therein"—that is, in this City of God and of the Lamb of Divine Sacrifice.

This is a world of superabundant selfishness, because it is a world of sin. The coming world shall be a world of living, loving Sacrifice because a world of Christ and His righteousness. *The wolf of greed will be replaced by the Lamb of God.* This is also a world of bloodshed. It has ever been so. In the coming world of Christ the Spirit of God will be shed abroad in the hearts and lives of all the Redeemed.

Chapter Six

THE BETTER COVENANT

Introduction

The term *"Berith,"* covenant, occurs in the Old Testament some three hundred times. Use of the covenant, however, extends to many peoples and to various relations of life. There are as many kinds of covenants as there are realms in which they function—social, political, commercial, professional, religious. An ordinary covenant is an agreement entered into in mutual confidence. Two or more persons may be party to it. For example, David and Jonathan had their covenant of friendship. So all Israel had their covenant with God. There is always a *nexus* or bond by which the covenant is enacted.

1. The Covenant of salt, thrice mentioned in the Old Testament, had virtue because of the sanctity of salt. It was known to be essential to life. Automatically on the parties partaking of salt the covenant came into existence. H. C. Trumbull relates how John Macgregor was captured on the upper Jordan by Arabs.[14] Taken to the sheik, he offered him some fine white salt. The sheik mistook it for sugar and tasted of

[14] The Covenant of Salt, p. 32.

it. Macgregor immediately did likewise. To the chagrin of the sheik he had to release the prisoner and restore all his belongings. The enactment of the covenant of salt had created a new relation and a right to be relied upon. Those enacting such a covenant pledged thereby friendship, honesty, protection and faithfulness to each other in all matters.

2. The English word "covenant" is the same in derivation as "convention," a coming together. But convention does not define the purpose of assembly. This coming together in covenant meant definite agreement, obligation, bond, treaty, compact, contract, promise, or pledge between two parties. "The Blood Covenant" was not confined to the religious realm. Here the bond was the mutual regard for the sacredness of blood as life itself. Usually the covenant was enacted by the partaking of each other's blood, or by a mingling of the two bloods, thus signifying or symbolizing a union of life. In the Old Covenant days the people furnished the blood of animals to be offered in covenant relation. In the New Covenant it was God who furnished the blood of His only begotten Son to signify this Covenant's sacrifice.

In passing we may note that each of the three great institutions, home, state and church, has its covenant. For the home there is the marriage covenant; for the state the covenant of citizenship, and for the church there is the covenant of faith. Any religion without a common faith tends to disintegrate. In any realm where there is regard for self only, no coherence is possible. "Every one for himself," creates no common attraction. The covenant shows regard for something beyond mere self.

3. All religious communions are held together by their unity of faith, devotion and worship. The Scottish Covenanters prized the object of their existence sufficiently to be called after it. Growing or changing religious faiths show this in change or development of covenant. Early in Old Testament days there was the Sabbath Covenant honoring the Creator and His work of Creation. There was the rainbow Covenant with Noah; the circumcision Covenant with Abraham, and the so-called Old Covenant with Moses and the Israelites. They were by it pledged as a Theocracy to obey the Divine laws—to be God's people, and He would be their God.

There are a great many phases of the New Covenant which concern us. In this chapter we shall begin by considering some of the ways in which it is a better covenant than the Old. It is better as a Covenant of Grace. It is better also in the substance which constitutes it. And better is it in the scope of its meaning as a covenant. This point, however, will need further discussion than that found in this chapter.

I. The Covenant of Grace Superior to That of Law

The New Covenant, because it is of Divine Grace, will ever remain new. It will never outgrow its name, for God's Grace has perpetual power of renewal and recovery. The great and only Redeemer who came in

Grace later announced: Rev. 21:5, "Behold I make all things new." This will have its consummation in "a new heaven and a new earth." The Messianic renewal in heart and spirit was thrice promised in Ezekiel—11:19, "And I will put a new spirit within you." 18:31, "Cast away from you all your transgressions, wherein ye have transgressed; and make you a new heart and a new spirit." 36:26, "A new heart also will I put within you; and I will take away the stony heart out of your flesh, and I will give you a heart of flesh."

1. In regard to the superiority of the Covenant of Grace the Epistle to the Hebrews takes no uncertain ground. It says: 8:6, "But now hath He (Christ) obtained a ministry the more excellent, by so much as He is also the Mediator of a better covenant which hath been enacted upon better promises." It says further: 8:13, "In that He saith, a new covenant, He hath made the first old. But that which is becoming old and waxeth aged, is nigh unto vanishing away." Between these two quotations is repeated perhaps the greatest of all the prophecies about this matter. It is Jeremiah 31:33 ff., and is worthy of being given here in full, for it is quoted three times in the Epistle:

> "Behold the days come, saith the Lord,
> That I will make a new covenant with the house of Israel and with the house of Judah;
> Not according to the covenant that I made with their fathers
> In the day that I took them by the hand to lead them forth out of the land of Egypt;
> For they continued not in my covenant,
> And I regarded them not, saith the Lord.
> For this is the covenant that I will make with

> the house of Israel after those days, saith the Lord;
> I will put my laws into their mind,
> And on their heart also will I write them:
> And I will be to them a God,
> And they shall be to me a people:
> And they shall not teach every man his fellow citizen,
> And every man his brother saying, Know the Lord:
> For all shall know me,
> From the least to the greatest of them,
> For I will be merciful to their iniquities,
> And their sins will I remember no more."

2. Taking up Grace as compared with Law, we may say that the superiority of the New Covenant does not mean that Law was abrogated. There is the new commandment or law of the Covenant of Grace: John 13:34, "A new commandment I give unto you, that ye love one another; even as I have loved you, that ye also love one another." There is also the living law of the New Covenant: Rom. 8:2, "The law of the Spirit of life in Christ Jesus made me free from the law of sin and of death." The Law of the Old Covenant remained as that of sonship in the likeness and image of God in which man was created. The primary essentiality of this law in creation has already been noted. The law of the relation of man to God's holy nature was not cancelled, nor could the law of necessary righteousness between man and man be abolished. *In the New Covenant a new and final way of attaining right relation between sinful man and God was found.* Never can it be superseded.

While there was no grace set forth in the law itself, there was grace in the very giving of the law that man might see and know his need of grace. The law would not be law in offering undeserved favors as Grace does, for the Divine commandment required what was due in man's relations to God and to fellow man. The law must of necessity announce what was right, what God regards as justice, what in righteousness was owed in all constituted relations and their obligations. Hence the Law was a pedagog to lead us to Christ by showing the chasm of sin into which man had fallen, and the need of gracious deliverance therefrom. The Law was a roadway, not an elevator like Grace. While it declared man's sinful condition and condemnation, it had no power to change them. On God's part whatever He promises, He counts that He owes.

When Grace is given big enough definition to take in "God in Christ," its superiority is written in the large. The law called on man for many sacrifices, but offered him none. The Covenant of Grace presents One Sacrifice so great that *all other needed sacrifices flow out of it.* Grace, however, is no blind generosity, but rather that specifically needed to save, to redeem, and sanctify. It met the need of a new foundation for personal righteousness, the living righteousness of life eternal.

3. The Law came by Moses; but Grace and Truth came by Him who is the Way, the Truth and the Life. That is the Way Divine Grace takes in the New Covenant. That is the Truth in Him who is God in Expression. That is the Life which sacrificed itself to replace

the living death of man with Life Eternal. Grace, combined with Truth as it is in Jesus, is the measure of the True Sacrifice of God that not only fully expresses the Sacrificial Divine Nature, but imparted to man would make his nature a fit expression of the sacrificial in response. Since Truth is always the realm of expression, in Grace as elsewhere, God uttered Himself in Truth by the personal sacrifice of Christ. Grace would not be Divine were it not the Divine Expression of the Godhead. And it would not be Truth unless it had the Divine hall-mark of being fully fitted for and permanently adapted to unending faith, for this is Truth's insignia from heaven. Grace is therefore the redeeming sacrifice needing only man's faith in it to work the miracle of his re-creation by and in Christ Jesus. Instead of bleeding the sinner, Grace bleeds for him.

The Covenant of Grace is the Divine down-reach to those sunken below the level of life, to lift them up into Divine favor, fellowship, and fulfilment—even to where they are purified and renewed, and related to righteousness as possessing it in Christ. The New Covenant is not temporary like the Old One, but is an abiding fulness of Grace that cannot be exhausted. All man's blessedness in eternity rests upon the stability of the Covenant of God's Grace to man in Christ.

II. The Better Substance of the New Covenant

For another thing the superiority of the New Covenant consists also in its substance. Law from God was the material and basis of the Old Covenant, but in the New *the substance is the Son of God in Person.* This was promised in prophecy. Concerning the Messiah, it was divinely announced through Isaiah 42:6, "I, Jehovah, will give thee for a covenant of the people." And again in 49:8, "Thus saith Jehovah . . . I will preserve thee, and give thee for a covenant of the people." The one so given could not be "suffering Israel," for the people could not be given to the people in covenant or in any other way, for they were not fit to save themselves, let alone any other. Israel has anything but fulfilled the place of "the suffering Servant," as depicted in prophecy. Israel has been the "suffering," but not the "servant."

1. That there was to be no Messiah but Israel itself, would render, as previously said, a great part of the Book of Isaiah meaningless. When Jesus read from Isaiah 61:1 ff., as to the day of the Lord in Messianic blessing, and said: "Today hath this Scripture been fulfilled in your ears," He was not mistaken in both interpretation and His personal fulfilment of the passage. Moreover, the Epistle to the Hebrews was not mistaken in its interpretation of Christ's fulfilment of the Messianic prophecies. They could apply to no one else. For example, Heb. 10: 5, 8, 19 and 20, "Sacrifice and offering thou wouldst not, but a body didst thou prepare for me; in whole burnt offerings and sacrifices for sin thou hadst no pleasure . . . (the which are offered according to the law), then hath He said, Lo, I am come to do thy will. He taketh away the first, that He may establish the second. By which will we

have been sanctified through the offering of the body of Jesus once for all. . . . Having therefore, brethren boldness to enter into the holy place by the blood of Jesus, by the way which He dedicated for us, a new and living way, through the veil, that is to say, His flesh." Also in Heb. 13:20, "Now the God of peace, who hath brought again from the dead the great shepherd of the sheep in the blood of an eternal covenant, even our Lord Jesus."

2. It may be remembered that in chapter four on the Personal Point of View there was set forth that our Redemption is grounded in the personal relations of the Godhead. Here we go a step further in pointing out that in substance the New Covenant is based on the bestowal of one of the Persons of the Holy Trinity. The Son of God is the means in Person of man's deliverance from sin. The oft quoted passage John 3:16 says, "God so loved the world that He gave His only begotten Son." The Epistle to the Hebrews opens with, "When He had made purification of sins, sat down on the right hand of the Majesty on high." Later, in 9:26, "But now once at the end of the ages hath He been manifested to put away sin by the sacrifice of Himself." Two verses later, "Christ having been once offered to bear the sins of many."

In these and similar passages there is clearly stated the superiority of the New Covenant over the Old, and this because its sacrifice is Christ in Person. The priests of the Old Covenant offered not themselves but animals, while Christ offered up Himself to God to blot out our sin. Had this personal substance of the sacrifice of Redemption been always given the first place, much confusion and error in interpreting the New Covenant would then have been avoided. Moral influence, eternal divine suffering, penitence, penalty, honor to God's Majesty, or to His government, and many other notions have been placed foremost as the substance of what was then called Christ's "atonement."

Our Lord occupies in the means of Redemption the same place that He does in the means of salvation. So the Word says. I Tim. 2:5, "For there is one God, and one Mediator between God and man, the man Christ Jesus." Tit. 2:14, "He gave Himself for us, that He might redeem us from all iniquity." I Thess. 5:9, "For God hath not appointed us to wrath, but to obtain salvation by our Lord Jesus Christ, who died for us, that whether we wake or sleep, we should live together with Him." Eph. 5:2, "Walk in love as Christ also hath loved us, and hath given Himself for us an offering and a sacrifice to God." Eph. 1:17, "In whom we have redemption through His blood, the forgiveness of sins, according to the riches of His grace."

3. Surely there should be no question about the Son of God being the efficient substance of Redemption, and that the seal or bond of the New Covenant is His blood, the Holy Scriptures and the Holy Spirit consistently bearing witness thereto. That His blood was shed in death, and that His death enabled Him to pour out His life ever since in a new and redeeming way, is as evident as that He became our brother in the flesh by means of the Incarnation.

The efficacy of His death was because it was in obedience to the Father; and it was the Christ of God who died. He was the Only One in all the world who could have given this sacrificial potency to death and *who received this power of self-impartation because of its efficacy.* That death was unique because He was unique—the only Godman (no hyphen in His Person) ever existing and dying for sinners. He stood in such strategic relations as no one else ever could stand; and into His death He brought all those relations and their potencies. Never before in any death was there such a converging of forces, of relations, of possibilities, of Godward efficacy and manward outreach. Because of the Son's integral place in the infinite and incomparable unity of the Trinity, He brought into that fateful, decisive struggle the Divine forces engaged in the conflict of heavenly unity with the disintegrating and disrupting forces of sin. What would Waterloo have been without Wellington? But this is no comparison whatever to what would Calvary have been without the Christ? There hundreds had been crucified in those cruel days; yet what pitiably little reach had the significance of their deaths! Still reach enough to call forth His crucifixion of death itself; for He

> "Bowed to the grave, destroyed it so,
> And death by dying, slew"

4. Before His passion in His heaven-enveloping and earth-encircling prayer, He said to the Father, "I have finished the work Thou gavest me to do." At the close of the agony of the Cross He said, "It is finished," and then dismissed His own spirit (Matt. 27:50). Here

the point to note is that nothing at all in the Old Covenant could compare with this personal process of self-realization by obedience to the Father and in self-fulfilment in His will. The colossal effect upon this colossal personality had taken place, by which the poured-out life for the Redemption of the world was thenceforth in operation of transmission, for the Crucified and Risen Person of the Christ had become the center and the circumference of the substance of the reservoir of redeeming efficacy of the New Covenant.

III. The New Covenant Better by Extended Meaning

Comparing the meaning of the Hebrew term *Berith* in the Old Testament with that of the Greek word *diathēkē* in the New Testament, we find that the latter came to have greatly extended meaning in the New Testament. The Hebrew word for covenant is derived from a verb meaning "to cut." "To cut a covenant" was an expression often used because the compact was originally enacted by the persons concerned passing between the two severed pieces of flesh thus cut in twain for the making of the covenant. In this way the bond of confederation or agreement came into being. The variations in the matters covenanted therewith, and the mutual forms of the *nexus* binding the contracting parties have already been discussed.

1. The Greek noun *diathēkē* comes from the corresponding verb, *diatithēmi,* meaning to make a covenant, to put apart, dispose in assignment, make a will, testament or bequeathment. The two parts of the

verb mean, *dia,* through; and *tithēmi,* to place, to put, to establish, to constitute. Here, then, is a reason for the New Covenant being considered better than the Old, because the latter meant simply compact, while the former meant both compact and bequeathment. Thayer says, "We find in the New Testament two distinct covenants spoken of, *duo diathēkai,* (Gal. 4:24), namely, the Mosaic and the Christian."[15] There was also the covenant with Abraham, an unconditional one (Gal. 3:7 ff).

The two parts of the Bible could have been called the Old and the New Covenants; but the word "Testament" belongs to the New and not to the Old. Both the Old and the New were covenants in the sense of *compact;* but the new only has instances of the added meaning of bequest as if by a will coming in force on the death of the testator. The New Covenant with this meaningful and immeasurably rich addition in substance is vastly superior to the Old. It has the infinite substance of a Divine-human Person given with all the riches of His resources and sacrificial achievement. We must study first His compact with the Father, then His bequeathment to believers.

2. The announcement of the Coming One appeared in the time of the Old Covenant and even before, but that promise was not made under it nor as part of it. This is clearly stated in Gal. 4: 4, 5: "When the fulness of the time came, God sent forth His Son, born of a woman, born under the law, that He might redeem them that were under the law, that we might receive

[15] **Greek-English Lexicon of the New Testament, p. 136.**

the adoption of sons." This shows us that the covenant was made long before it was fulfilled when Messiah came. In the preceding chapter it is shown that the promise of the New Covenant was made to Abraham. Gal. 3:8 ff., "And the scripture, foreseeing that God would justify the Gentiles (nations) by faith, preached the gospel beforehand unto Abraham, saying, "In thee shall all the nations be blessed . . . that upon the Gentiles might come the blessing of Abraham in Jesus Christ." In this whole section three very important things are announced: *First,* the covenant gift of the Son—that God would send forth the Spirit of His Son into our hearts. This is really the two other things in the bequeathment, *second,* regeneration; and *third,* the gift of the indwelling Spirit. This pertinent passage is important enough to quote in full, Gal. 3:15 ff.

> "Brethren, I speak after the manner of men: Though it be but a man's covenant, yet when it hath been confirmed, no one maketh it void, or addeth thereto. Now to Abraham were the promises spoken, and to his seed. He saith not, and to seeds, as of many; but as of one (Gen. 13:15). And to thy seed, which is Christ. Now this I say: A covenant confirmed beforehand by God, the law, which came four hundred and thirty years after, doth not disannul, so as to make the promise of none effect. For if the inheritance is of the law, it is no more of promise; but God hath granted it to Abraham by promise. What then is the law? It was added because of transgressions, till the seed should come to whom the promise hath been made. . . . But the scripture shut up all things under sin, that the promise by faith in Jesus Christ might be given to them that believe. . . . For ye are all sons of God, through faith, in Christ Jesus."

3. When the *covenanted promise* of the coming of the Son took place, is one thing; when the *covenanted*

coming of the Son came to pass, is another. The inauguration of the New Covenant in its first half was by the Incarnation. The Covenant promise was made to His mother. Luke 1:31, "And behold thou shalt conceive in thy womb, and bring forth a Son, and shalt call His name Jesus. He shall be great, and shall be called the Son of the Most High: and the Lord God shall give unto Him the throne of His father David; *and He shall reign over the house of Jacob for ever; and of His kingdom there shall be no end.*" Every child by his coming is a covenant with God; but the coming of the King's Son from heaven is the fulfilment of God's covenant with Abraham in the Divine life given. There could not be God's bequeathment covenant fulfilled in the giving of His Son to man as Saviour, without there being God's covenant with the Son, even that Son who was in Himself a covenant in both senses of compact and bequeathment. If ever one came not for his own sake, that One was He who came for our sakes. God's covenant with Him was therefore that He would be with Him and never fail Him in all His incarnate life. He did depend on the Father and the Holy Spirit that His mission would not fail, the greatest mission ever undertaken; and that His sacrifice would not be in vain, the greatest sacrifice ever offered. Thus would be fulfilled the greatest of all covenants; and thus would be consummated the greatest of all fulfilments.

CHAPTER SEVEN

THE NEW COVENANT IN TWOFOLD MEANING

INTRODUCTION

IN this chapter we approach the apex of the argument. Calvary represents the summit of sacrifice where the Redeemer laid down His life. The zenith was reached in heaven when its Holy of Holies was entered, and the Great High Priest offered Himself to God as the personal means of our Redemption. Then and there the New Covenant was enacted and "The Heart of the New Testament" was made manifest.

1. Up to this point we have considered the first half of the Covenant of our Redemption. Its accepted offering was made. Next comes the mediation of its merit. Its efficacy with God secured its efficiency with sinners. The fulfilment of God's holy nature provided the means for the fulfilment of man's nature. This shows the Covenant of Redemption to be not only compact with God, but also bequeathment, testament, or will in favor of man.

2. This personal Redemption in Christ is both unique and incomparable, as unique and incomparable as Christ Himself. The New Covenant is so extraordinary,

it best manifests the very heart of God. The Mosaic covenant had its human conditions and temporal sacrifices, while the New Covenant was by the everlasting sacrifice of the Eternal Son by the eternal spirit of the Trinity in which compact the Great High Priest is both the Sacrifice and the Offerer. Because its merit was infinite in Christ, it is perpetual.

3. In the second phase of this New Covenant the Redeemer is both Testator and Bequeathment. As man's Re-Creator He imparts Himself in nature free from and victorious over sin. He reproduces in man sacrificial character and spiritual life identified with His own. He wills Himself to us, makes Himself the Executor of His own will, and by submitting to death brings the will into force. Rising from the dead, He is the only Testator in all history who served as the Executor of His own will—and this the Will of all wills!

I. THE MEANING OF *Diathēkē* IN THE EPISTLE TO THE HEBREWS

That the word "covenant" has this twofold meaning depends in part upon the meaning we find in the Greek original. It is true that in the Old Testament *Berith* had the single meaning of reciprocal compact or agreement. It is also true that in early or classical Greek the corresponding term, *diathēkē*, had up till the first century the similar single meaning, except in the Abrahamic covenant. The reason for this solitary exception is—the New Covenant in Christ was *the Abrahamic Covenant in fulfilment.* This was God's unconditional covenant with Abraham that as his seed Christ should come (Gal. 3:16). Beyschlag interprets the second meaning a mere play on the term "covenant." Westcott endeavers to hold the word in question to the same restricted meaning all through the Epistle. Principal Edwards in the Expositor's Bible looks upon the second meaning of *diathēkē* as merely used in illustration. Many other good authorities could be cited as sharing in the same refusal to give the larger interpretation or translation to this word "covenant."

1. All these objections may be refuted on the grounds of both internal and of external evidence. For example, the writer of Hebrews would not in that case have argued the necessity of death to bring this covenant into force. That is true of a will or bequeathment covenant only. The writer says, "There must of necessity be the death of him that made it;" and the *diathēkē* "doth never avail while he that made it, liveth." Moses did not have to die to bring the Mosaic Covenant into effect; nor did his death in the least affect it in any way. Only a bequeathment covenant fits the facts of all the writer of the Epistle to the Hebrews says on this matter. All the opponents to the compact-bequeathment view overlook a very important possibility, namely that this word like many others might change in meaning, take on new or added significance. Fortunately there is overwhelming amount of evidence that contemporary business language, the *Koine*, did this very thing, used this term mainly in the bequeathment sense.

2. Let us next consult an up-to-date Greek dictionary

and other authorities. Thayer's Greek-English Lexicon says as to the meaning of the term in question: "Finally must be noted the amphiboly or twofold use by which the writer to the Hebrews, in 9:16 sq. substitutes for the meaning *covenant* which *diathēkē* bears elsewhere in the Epistle that of testament, and likens Christ to a testator." [16]

In the latest (ten volumes) edition of Liddell and Scott we find *diathēkē* translated as: "Disposition of property by will. With *kata*—by will." [17]

In the *Oxyrhynchus Papyri*, arranged and translated by Grenfell and Hunt, we find very large numbers of wills, revocation of wills, and registration of inheritances, dated near the very beginning of the second century. These papyri use the term *diathēkē* over and over again to express the words "will" or "testament."

Scholars realize today, because of these vastly important discoveries in the *Koine* literature of this early period, that previous classical Greek usage cannot determine finally the meaning of a New Testament term. Inspiration was not compelled to patronize classical Greek meanings exclusively. That the current usage of *diathēkē* in New Testament days meant covenant in or by *testament* or *will*, may be taken as fully established by the testimony of the tons, the very large amounts of papyri dug up in Egypt since 1900.

3. There is also another line of corroboration—in Paul's Epistle to the Galatians. This is well brought

[16] Page 137—Corrected Edition, 1893.
[17] Greek-English Lexicon, New Edition, 1927.

out by C. T. Wood in his "Life, Letters and Religion of St. Paul." He says:

(Galatians 3:15, 23, Introductory Note). This section is difficult. In order to understand it, we must bear in mind that *diatheke* (covenant) was used (1) for a covenant, in the sense of a contract between two parties, binding on both, as the Law was; (2) for a last will and testament, disposing of one's property at death, i.e., an unconditional gift or promise. St. Paul insists that God's promises to Abraham were absolutely unconditioned by His observance of any Law: they were a free and irrevocable gift. *But Genesis 15:18 calls them a diatheke* (O.T. in Greek) (covenant). Yes, says the Apostle, but this was not a contract with conditions attached; it was like a will, giving an inheritance without conditions. The Mosaic Law was a contract; but as it was not given till 430 years after the "covenant," it cannot annul the latter . . . Now there is a complete difference between the two common forms of "testament," namely, a legal contract and gift by will: one is a covenant, resting on legal conditions which bind both parties; the other is a free promise binding only him who makes it. The second is what God in His goodness gave to Abraham.[18]

If, therefore, this holds good in the Epistle to the Galatians, surely it also holds good equally in the Epistle to the Hebrews.

4. Dr. R. W. Dale says:

To my own mind, it seems certain that, although the word bears the sense of "covenant" everywhere else in the Epistle, and everywhere else in the New Testament, it means here, what it means most frequently in ordinary Greek writers,—the disposition or arrangement of property by a testament.[19]

And there is profound truth hinted at in the sudden transi-

[18] C. T. Wood, Fellow and Dean of Queens' College, Cambridge, pp. 81, 82. T. & T. Clark, Edinburgh, Publishers.

[19] **The Jewish Temple and the Christian Church,** p. 218. (It is to Dr. Dale's credit that he came to his conclusion in this matter quite a number of years before the discovery of the Egyptian papyri.)

tion in the meaning of the term. It is not a mere play on words. The new relation between God and man may be justly regarded as resting rather on a will than on a covenant. In a covenant there are conditions to be fulfilled on both sides. The terms require fidelity from both parties. But the inheritance we hope for, hardly seems to depend on our fulfilling the conditions of a proper covenant. There is no proportion between what God requires of us, and what He intends to bestow. The inheritance is a free gift; it has to be received with gratitude rather than purchased by obedience. It is like what comes to us by the terms of a will, rather than what we secure by fulfilling the provisions of a bond.[20]

II. Examination of the New Covenant in Hebrews

Ours is the Great God of adequate means for His desires and purposes. Human redemption requires nothing less than Divine personal means. So He sent and prepared His only begotten Son by the Incarnation, His earthly life, death by sin and resurrection from the dead. Thus He became the personal Fount of Redemption to give His risen, re-creative life in the New Covenant. It is both interesting and instructive to examine the five mentions of this New Covenant as they occur in the Epistle to the Hebrews.

1. The first is in 8:8, "I will make (accomplish) a New Covenant." This is to be recorded not only in the Scriptures but also in human hearts; for by it is to come the impartation of new life, new nature, new relation to God, and new knowledge of Him Who said, "For all shall know me from the least to the greatest of them" (8:11). The whole section of this prophecy quoted from Jeremiah 31:31 ff. is a comparison of the two covenants. The new is called the

[20] **The Jewish Temple and the Christian Church,** p. 219.

better covenant enacted upon better promises. "For if that first covenant had been faultless, then would no place have been sought for a second."

2. The next reference is 8:13, the commentary at the conclusion of the prophecy above referred to. It is as follows: "In that He saith, a new covenant, He hath made the first old. But that which is becoming old and waxeth aged is nigh unto vanishing away." This shows what has already been said, that the Old Covenant mainly consisted in conditional compact, contract, or mutual agreement between God and His people in the matter of their obedience to laws and directions given by Him.

On the other hand the New Covenant is both unconditional and certified bequeathment. It is compact between the Son and the Father that the former would perfectly fulfil the Father's will in sacrifice of Himself for sinners. "By the obedience of the One shall the many be made righteous." This was realized by "eternal spirit" perpetuating in Him and imparting forever this personal sacrifice of Christ. He is the substance and soul of this incomparable offering to God and at the same time the bequeathment part of the New Covenant requiring that He impart Himself to believers.

3. The next mention of the New Covenant is in 9:15 ff. "He is the Mediator of a new covenant (marg. testament also), that a death having taken place for the redemption (in the matter) of transgressions that were under the first covenant, they that have been

called, may receive the promise of the eternal inheritance. For where a testament (will) is, there must of necessity be (brought) the death of him that made it. For a testament (will) is of force where there hath been death (Gr., over the dead); for it doth never avail while he that made it liveth."

In verses 11 to 14 of the preceding section its conclusion is based on the fact that Christ as High Priest entered by His own blood[21] into the Holy of Holies in the very presence of God once for all in (or by) eternal spirit, the spirit of the entire sacrificial Godhead. The offering being thus eternally perfect, the Redemption secured is likewise for eternity. Had the passage said, "by the eternal spirit," it would have meant the Holy Spirit. He as Author of the Word, has meaning as truly by what He leaves out as by what He puts in. In the original text there is no article before "eternal spirit."

4. The fourth reference is indirectly to the New Covenant, but directly to the New and Living Way in it. This is its *access*. The passage is 10:19, 20. "Having therefore, brethren, boldness to enter into the holy place by the blood of Jesus, by the way which He dedicated for us, a new and living way, through the veil, that is to say His flesh; and having a great priest over the house of God, let us draw near with a true heart in fulness of faith."

So we turn to *access*, not to further argument. The argument is concluded. That ended with the remission

[21] That this blood must have been the spiritual life of the resurrection body, the spiritual blood of Christ's spiritual or risen body is discussed at the close of the next chapter, the eighth. The inference is that this blood is eternal.

of sins being established. He Who is the living Way, the personal Truth, and the sacrificial Life, has led us by the Truth in Himself to this access into God's immediate presence by the new and living Way through or in the Sacrifice of the New Covenant. Hitherto He has been called a higher Melchizedek, the King Priest, the High Priest, the great High Priest, but is here named simply, "a great priest over the house of God." This greatness lies in that great power or ability He has for cleansing, the cleansing from all sin by an absolutely new and unique means, His life-blood with its potency to blot out sin, to blot it out of existence. There is His shed blood by which He entered the Holy of Holies in the very presence of God for us and to admit us there; and there is the cleansing blood for each personally flowing from His open wounds, keeping on cleansing us as John says (I John 1:7). Thus He met the constitutional and the operative necessity for our Redemption by the New Covenant.

Among very many excellent things of great spiritual helpfulness the Christian Hebrew, Adolph Saphir, has summarized our fourfold assurance in this matter — "Eternal redemption; access to God; consciences purged by the blood of Christ to serve the living God; and the heirship blessings in Heavenly places."[22]

There remains this to be said: when we come to God with His Word in our minds, and our hearts cleansed by that which removes consciousness of sin, we are able then not only to stand, but to remain through this

[22] **The Epistle to the Hebrews,** Vol. II, p. 576.

New and Living Way in the immediate presence of the Living and True God. Iniquity, the one great obstacle, has been removed. The one great desire to be there has come into fulfilment. And through imparted life, oneness of nature, affinity with God and nearness to Him make us satisfied as no other place can.

5. The fifth and last mention of the New Covenant in this Epistle is in 12:24, "But ye are come . . . to Jesus the mediator of a new covenant, and to the blood of sprinkling that speaketh better than (that of) Abel." A similar passage is in I Peter 1:2, "According to the foreknowledge of God the Father, in sanctification of the Spirit, unto obedience and sprinkling of the blood of Christ."

Seven important things have been mentioned, of which these are the last two. Twice we have briefly discussed the mediatorship of Christ. In offering, Christ is High Priest; in covenant relation He is Mediator; and in rulership He is King, Head of the Kingdom of God. But this is not all His titles; and every title has its correspondence in greatness of relation and place.

As Westcott has pointed out, this is the only instance in the New Testament where *nea* is used with the word "covenant." Elsewhere it is *kainē* which is employed. Both of these terms mean "new," but the first signifies new in the sense of *recent existence;* and the other means new in *character and substance.* So in this case it is "*a* new covenant," not "*the* new covenant." The Old Covenant called for many sacrifices. The New called for but one and its consummation in impartation or bequeathment.

In this passage contrast is also drawn between the blood of Abel crying out from the ground for vengeance, and the sprinkled blood of the Mediator of this New Covenant that speaketh better things than that by the blood of the slain brother. What it speaks is not said; and yet we know that it speaks remission, forgiveness, redemption. God's silence is often louder than our utterance. Abel's blood was physical. The sprinkled blood of the Mediator and Sacrifice of the New Covenant could not have been merely physical. If flesh and blood in a material order could not inherit the Kingdom of God, how could such physical blood go into that spiritual Kingdom, the heavenly Holy of Holies, to purchase inheritance for others? This we shall endeavor to explain, if it can be explained, in the next chapter. But first we must finish our examination of the occurrences of the expression, "the New Covenant," elsewhere in the New Testament than in the Epistle to the Hebrews.

III. The New Covenant in the Rest of the New Testament

From what has been already said as to the important place of the New Covenant in the Epistle to the Hebrews, some may take it that this expression is confined to that portion of the Scriptures. We have only to recall that the New Testament is but another name for the New Covenant, just as the Old Testament is merely another name for the Old Covenant. On examination we find that all three of the Synoptic Gospels make use of it, and that Paul mentions it in both of his Epistles to the Corinthians. So far as the whole New Testament is concerned, the New Covenant is central in its interpretation of Christ's Redemption.

1. We find that these words, "the New Covenant," were first uttered by the lips of the Lord Himself in explaining the significance of the Lord's Supper. He said of the wine as its symbol, "This is my blood of the new covenant." Matthew and Mark have precisely the same words. Luke varies from them but agrees with Paul in quoting, "This cup is the new covenant in my blood." In the Gospels the references are, Matt. 26:28, Mark 14:24, Luke 22:20.

Baptism setting forth the beginning of the Christian life through the Saviour's death, burial and resurrection, and spiritually the believer's similar death to sin, burial in separation from the world and resurrection to walk in newness of life, takes place but once with no need of repetition. The Lord's Supper witnessing two great effects of the New Covenant, the constant cleansing by the blood of Christ and the continual nourishment of the believer by Christ as the Bread of Life, are to be repeated over and over again in the testimony of the Church. Both of these ordinances are more than testimony of faith in Christ; they are expressions of His interpretation as to the soul and substance of the New Covenant relation and operation. Who better understood its genesis and genius?

2. Turning to the two passages in which Paul makes specific mention of the New Covenant, we find the

same profound and fundamental agreement with the Epistle to the Hebrews on this matter. First he explains the source of what he says: "For I received of the Lord that which I delivered unto you." In I Cor. 11:25 he goes on to repeat the same interpretation as that of Luke: "This cup is the new covenant in my blood." Though the whole Word of God has no more profound thinker than this great Apostle, he does not depend on his own understanding. On any matter when giving merely his own judgment, he says so plainly. Hence he repeats what the Lord had told him about the communion of the Lord's Supper inspired by Christ's own interpretation of it, and this accounts for the perfect agreement among all the New Testament writers not only as to the New Covenant itself but also as to every thing in word or deed, in ordinance or other observance. The grip of its vital conception and relation, produced by the Holy Spirit's ministry in the out-working of this living, always active relation of the covenant, controlled what was said. In this way the most ordinary mind controlled by Christ in this covenant relation was more dependable than that of the greatest genius without Him.

In II Cor. 2:6 Paul is further explaining how in this blessed covenant impartation to us, "our sufficiency is of God." He makes clear, this is because of what the New Covenant does for us and through us in Christ: "Who also made us sufficient as ministers of a new covenant." This reminds us of Hebrews 12:24 where Christ is represented as "the Mediator of a new covenant." Paul is here dealing with the New Covenant's practical outcome in Christian service undivorced from the cause of Christ. He goes on to explain that this is "a ministration of righteousness," exceeding in glory that of the Old Covenant, for its glory was passing away. He maintains that the ministration of the New Covenant cannot be other than glory, because of the Holy Spirit. To sum up, having received the Christ of the New Covenant by the ministry of the Spirit, by the same ministry and in it we are made sufficient ministers of Christ to others.

Chapter Eight

THE BLOOD'S FUNCTION IN REDEMPTION

Introduction

In Chapter Three we considered "The Blood As a Symbol of Sacrifice." These captions lie close to each other. The blood may be considered as constitutionally sacrificial in its service to life. God has given it this place. He has also given the blood of the Redeemer its place. It will be our task to discuss its service in the process of Redemption.

1. Here we may note how its place in the Incarnate life of Christ led to its service in redeeming sinners. The Creator instituted human life by breathing the breath of life (Heb. lives) into man's divinely formed body. It is a long way from there to where the Re-Creator breathed the breath of His risen life into the spiritual lives of the startled disciples in the upper room on that first Easter evening. That instituted a new day for them.

We shall not be able to explain everything in this matter, just as we cannot explain how the uncreated Creator became a Creature in the Virgin's womb.

There, as we have already showed, the embryo formed the heart, then the large blood vessels, then the blood. Here biological terms are most fitting. Metaphysics talks in abstract terms; and abstraction is the great curse of theology. Biologically that blood of the Incarnate One physically and vitally represented the union of the Divine-human life. The Word being made flesh included the blood-life within it.

Was ever blood so meaningful and sacred, so potent and precious? It was more than the physical basis of the united Incarnate life of God the Son. It was a vital visibilation of the fact of the sacrificial nature of God taking on blood-relation with sinful men and undertaking their redemption. In that blood pulsed the fulness of the Father's love and grace. That life-blood of the Incarnate Son was of a kind sacrificially with the Spirit of the whole Godhead. In that eternal sacrificial spirit of the Trinity Christ came that He might offer up Himself to meet man's need of redemption. That blessed blood of His physical life had ministered to His soul as well as His body, and thus to His spirit and Deity conjoined with His humanity.

2. There was an infinitely far-sighted strategy in God's great plan of redemption, when He permitted the powers of evil unwittingly to open up by the crucifixion the infinite personal reservoir of sacrificial Divine life in the Incarnate One. God never permits sin in the sense that He sanctions it; but He could not but permit the possibility of sin when He gave to personality its essential power of self-determination. That

freedom of self-realization might be and was abused in turning away from Him, and making something else the end of existence, giving to it the place that God alone is fit to fill, we plainly see.

Little did any or all of those who had to do with the crucifixion of Christ, realize what they were doing. Further than succeeding in putting Him away they could not see. That this might eventuate in putting away the very thing which inspired them to kill Him, was utterly beyond their nature and power to see. But the Divine mind and purpose saw that the very wounds of Christ's Person would become outlets to enable the Redeemer's life to pour itself out, and so to contact sin as to destroy it forever.

I. The Light of Scripture on Redemption's Effect

Personal life has carried sin and its effect in many directions. Redemption must be in every direction it has taken. Man must be cured of his ungodliness, from all godlessness. Selfishness at the root of all outward manifestations, and inhumanity always due to failure toward God and selfishness within need final remedy.

1. Perhaps the clearest of all interpretations of the mystery of the mastery of the power of the blood of Christ to blot out sin comes from the Mind of Inspiration back of, and in the light of, the Scriptures.

Beginning with Heb. 9:26, "But now once at the end of the ages hath He been manifested to put away sin by the sacrifice of Himself." In the original there is but one word for "to put away," and it is very much stronger in the Greek. It is not a verb, but a noun, *athetēsis*. It is governed by the preposition *eis*, usually meaning unto. Instead of "to put away sin" it should read, to the end of obliteration (or annihilation) of sin. The same word occurs in 7:18, and is there translated, "For there is a *disannuling* of the foregoing commandment." This term *athetēsis* is one of the strongest words which the Greek language affords, meaning a rendering void, extermination, utter abolition. So God speaks in very strong terms as to what is done with sin.

Next, Rev. 1:5, "Unto Him that loveth us, and loosed (or washed) us from our sins by (in) His blood." Here the verb for loosed is *lusanti*, from *louō*, meaning to wash.

I John 3:5, "And ye know that He was manifested to take away sins." Here "to take away" is the translation of *airō*, which means take or put away, remove, bear, or expiate.

I John 1:7, "And the blood of Jesus His Son cleanseth us from all sin." The verb here is *katherizō*, and the form used *katherizei*, historical present, meaning keeps on cleansing, purifying, or purging.

Acts 22:16, "Arise and be baptized, and wash away thy sins." The verb here is the same as in Rev. 1:5 except that it is intensified with *apo*, *apolouō*; form used *apolousai*, meaning cleanse fully, or have remitted.

Acts 3:19, "Repent ye therefore, and turn again, that your sins may be blotted out." Here also we come across another very strong word. It is *exaleiphō*, which also means to wipe out, to exterminate.

2. As we have been giving special attention to the Epistle to the Hebrews in the matter of Covenant Redemption, it may be well to note here that in it Christ's death is mentioned not nearly so frequently as His blood. Six times His death is spoken of, and the blood twenty-two times. The more frequent emphasis is on the blood and the ideas it conveys. Some may object that the blood always means His death; but this is scarcely true. "The blood is the life," sounds out in the Scriptures from the very first. In Leviticus 17: 11, 14, "for the life of the flesh is in the blood." Certainly the Epistle to the Hebrews does not ignore the death of Christ or its meaning. In emphasizing the priesthood of Christ, the New Covenant, and Redemption by it, the blood as a term is of more use to express how the sacrifice of Christ was made, as He offered Himself in the Holy of Holies, and to portray how in self-giving the Redeemer cleanses the sinner from his sins.

II. How Christ's First Blood-Life Was Ended

It may appear strange to some that the Eternal Son should take on the temporal, physical and mortal nature in the Incarnation; but He was uniting with human nature as it is in all but its sin. Since Jesus Christ was God come in human flesh and blood, then His blood-life was that in the body of His Incarnate Person. Physical blood is not naturally immortal. What became of the blood-life of Enoch and Elijah who were translated, we are not told. Nor do we know exactly what shall become of the blood-life of the persons who at the Lord's

Second Coming will be changed into another body in a moment. While the Son of God was passing through the intense suffering and humiliation on the cross His body lived by its blood-life until death's release intervened.

By His Incarnation God prepared the Redeemer a body, that through it and its possibilities of sacrifice in death He might become fully equipped in Person to pour out His redeeming life for the blotting out or destruction of iniquity. As already said, there was needed sin's wounding and death-dealing effects to enable the completion of the sacrifice of Himself unto God and for man. Only by the Divine taking human life and nature into union with itself could the Person of Christ become tangible to sin and vulnerable to death at the hand of iniquity. Because this brought to pass His being "wounded for our transgressions," He came into the necessary contact with sin to prepare and enable His Person to destroy it finally, root and branch, in human Persons. It was therefore the nature and location of sin in human personality which made necessary Christ's death to contact it and thus destroy it.

1. In II Cor. 13:4 the Holy Spirit by Saint Paul said: "For He was crucified through weakness," the weakness of a mortal human body. In 12:10 in the previous chapter it was said, "For when I am weak, then am I strong." So He became strong to destroy sin through the weakness of a mortal human body and by suffering the sacrifice in death which prepared Him for redeeming self-impartation. Thus His redemptive

omnipotence as God was made perfect in human weakness. Thus supplied the necessary condition in His Divine-human Person of being wounded, bruised, crucified and slain, that out of the very wounds in His risen body there might flow out the redeeming, sin-destroying life for sinful man. And for that very reason these wounds in His body must remain unhealed till the world's Redemption is accomplished and the last soul saved.

So it came to pass that our Lord was put to a physical death, the only kind possible to God incarnate. Could He have been put to death spiritually, then His self-impartation, if any, would have been of spiritual death. The Father could raise His body when dead, but He could not raise the Son from spiritual death, for then the Father would be as dead to Him as He would be to the Father. And so two dead, separated deities instead of One Living God would have no power to raise each other. Peter discriminates as to the character of the death the Redeemer died (I Peter 3:18) "Because Christ also suffered for sins once, the righteous for the unrighteous, that He might bring us to God, being put to death in the flesh, but made (kept) alive in the spirit." Or made alive in supernatural, spiritual, resurrection life.

2. What became of the blood-life of Christ? When poured out, of course, it died, and He died. After His resurrection He said to His disciples, "A spirit (ghost, apparition) hath not flesh and bones as ye see me have." This was to convince those who saw Him in

His resurrection body that He was *reality* and identity in body as well as in soul and spirit. He did not say "blood and flesh" (the Greek order), for His blood had died, but His changed flesh was alive, living by some other higher means. Now all life is essentially spirit. This is its substance: this is what it is in its innermost. At its deepest physical life is spirit integrated or organized in matter, in "physical body." At death the life, soul, or spirit leaves its body, that is, the spiritual then dissociates itself from the physical Christ's blood could no longer function in life because its life-spirit had gone out from it. So to speak, the soul of every living corpuscle had forsaken it. When His heart broke and He died, all His blood shared in that death of deaths. Not a drop of it was still alive.

The human soul is that part of the human spirit which is vitally organized in the human body. When Jesus died both soul and spirit left all direct contact and relation to His body. It was no swoon, as some have suggested. On the third day He came back to His body, the same body, and yet *far from being the same* in nature, power and life. Men have been saying that no two material existences can occupy the same space at the same time. This is true of much physical material; and it was true of Jesus' body before He died and up to the time of His resurrection. Then it became the first resurrection body, a new order of physical existence, no doubt the very highest type possible in matter, like ether and cosmic rays. It could come through closed doors; it could appear and then disappear. The needs and properties of the ordinary human body seem to have been vastly transcended. This new body was in reality more like spirit than like ordinary matter. Yet it could be touched and handled. It has been found that the substance called ether is structureless and atomless. Some one has said that it is little more than a noun for the verb "to vibrate." Not long ago it would have been maintained that such a type of inter-existent matter could not be. Then there are the cosmic rays, with still other strange properties. Surely we have today little scientific room to deny the reality and character of the resurrection body in the presence of these super-physical entities or high orders of material substance.

Hitherto we have been holding that matter is electrodynamic, ions and corpuscles of force. According to this view it is simply stored up energy. When He created matter, instead of by magic fiat God made it out of His measureless might. That is a sacrificial origin. It cost much even to His almightiness. Some think it came by a divine magic, namely, that all God needed to do was to utter a fiat, the mere words, "Let be!" and forthwith the worlds and the universe sprang into existence. God does not create quite so cheaply as that. All creation by God involves His sacrificial expenditure.

The Son was the Divine Instrument of Creation, the Father being the Source. He later found Himself in fashion as a man, or was made in the likeness of sinful man. A body was given unto Him with which to serve God and suffer for man. As the slave-master pierced the slave's ear by pinning it to the doorpost in token of ownership, so was the Son of God given a body to be pierced by the crucifixion as a slave to sacrificial Divine love, that man's need of Redemption might be provided or purchased in His Person. Perhaps the Septuagint translators of the Hebrew Old Testament did not do such poor work after all on this passage. See Ps. 40: 6 ff. and Heb. 10: 5 ff.

III. How the Redeemer's Blood-Life Was Replaced

The triumphant, majestic miracle of Christ's resurrection is like that of His Incarnation, for both are utterly beyond our power to explain. Did we know the secret of the supernatural process of miracles, we might then be able to perform them. While Christ could not share with anyone on earth the mystery of the miracle of His supernatural conception, He is going to share with all the redeemed the miracle of His resurrection. Miraculous redemption—bodies are not promised to the unsaved. The term resurrection as applied to lost souls cannot mean that they are to be given redemption of their bodies. How would unredeemed souls fit redeemed bodies?

We are promised that because the Redeemer arose, we too shall arise, or be changed in a moment to the new body at His coming. Even though we die, we shall not need the scattered, decayed dust of the buried bodies, for we are definitely told: "Thou sowest (buriest) not the body that shall be." Yet people who profess to believe the Bible are burying billions of dollars on cemetery preservation of the dust of the dead.

Would not all that money count for more, if spent in evangelizing the millions who have never heard of the Gospel and its resurrection?

1. When Christ rose from the dead, in Him two great changes took place—His body was transformed and a higher means of life instituted within it. The first body was adapted to the kind of life He first lived, and was mortal. It was suited to soul-life (*psuchikon soma*). The superior resurrection body was fitted to spirit-life (*pneumatikon soma*). The latter is an immortal body not necessarily confined to this physical world. When the terms "spiritual body" and "spiritual blood" are used, this does not mean body and blood made of spirit (a contradiction in terms), but rather adapted to spiritual life. There is a profound difference between this adaptation of body and blood to spiritual life and that adapted to soul life of the natural realm. They are as different as the immortal resurrection body is from the mortal body of the physical realm. The two former are adapted to the higher life and nature of the spirit realm and are without the limitations of life belonging to the natural physical world.

Rom. 8:23 says: "We wait for our adoption, to wit, the redemption of our body." The Scriptures tell us in more than one place that, "God raised up Jesus Christ." But Rom. 6:4 and Gal. 1:1 say that the Father raised Him up. And Rom. 8:11 says that the Holy Spirit raised Him up. John 2:19 records that Christ said He Himself would raise up the temple of His body. In this as in all other things performed by the Godhead, the Father and the Holy Spirit are absolutely inseparable co-workers with the Son. The Persons of the Holy Trinity live and act in such perfect unity that there is complimentary coöperation of all Three as transcendent as the Godhead Itself.

2. On that first Easter evening the Risen Saviour appeared in the midst of the disciples in the room where they had gathered. He who was the "Door" to Life Eternal, now needed not the service of any door to enter a room; and no door was opened. Naturally they were startled by this supernatural entrance. As John 20: 21 ff. relates it, "Jesus said to them again, Peace be unto you. . . . And when He had said this, He breathed on them, and said unto them, Receive ye the Holy Spirit."

For one thing, here was absolute proof of His Deity; for only God can give the Spirit of God. For another matter, there was the Lord's identification of Himself, and the revelation of the mystery how He lived in His risen body. In the act of imparting to them the Holy Spirit by breathing on them, He showed not only that the Holy Spirit had become the very breath of life to His Risen body, but had become the life-imparting Inhabitant of it. When at the creation of man God breathed into him "the breath of lives" (lit. livings), blood, soul and spirit came into existence and co-operation. Thus God gave man what no animal ever had, the human spirit which is the seat of personality with its capacity for God.

The inhabitation and impartation of the Holy Spirit

are thus normal to man where there is no sin. When Christ's body was put to death by sin, it laid a portion of three days in the grave, till that Easter morning He rose from the tomb, more than victorious over the work and death of sin; and in the changed, risen, supernatural body He resumed His incarnate form of life. One might almost say — super-incarnate life. His supernatural-resurrection body was made alive and lived by the Spirit of the Resurrection; and by that same Holy Spirit His body still lives today and moves and manifests Him when and where He wills so to do.

Being fully convinced of His identity of body, soul, and spirit, the disciples must have wondered how He was living in a body which had been dead almost three days, and whence it had so changed as to flash through solid walls, then disappear again. They had seen Him raise the dead who resumed their former physical life as before with bodies unchanged in life and nature. Here was the Risen One before them in a uniquely new sort of body more like spirit than like His former body. This body could not be animated by ordinary blood; but must have taken on higher means of life suited to its risen, supernatural character. True, He had the indwelling Spirit without measure all the days of His flesh. Now in this higher body, more adapted to the very Spirit of God, how does it live? Manifestly by the same Holy Spirit, not only as breath and life, but also the Holy Spirit must have taken up the work of His blood-life, and become the "spiritual" blood (so to speak) that animated His risen body.[23] This would be normal to the Holy Spirit as specially fitted to take on the blood-function of the risen, "spiritual" body of the Redeemer. He who functioned in the Miraculous Conception of the Incarnation, when the blood-life of the Incarnate One became possible, could minister to the need of life-sustenance and perpetual maintenance in Jesus' risen body.

3. Elsewhere I have pointed out that each inter-existent Person of the Trinity has His trinity of offices. For the Holy Spirit these are, impartation, fellowship and fulfilment. In the Father—sovereignty, source and plan or purpose. In the Son—manifestation, creation (agent) and sacrifice in person. (*Personality and the Trinity*, pp. 135, 163, 196.) How well all these Divine functions fit together in Redemption! Henceforth living in a body alive by the impartation-life of the Holy Spirit from the Source in the Father, the Crucified and Risen One may by the Holy Spirit impart Himself as Infinite Redeemer in unlimited measure of ministry.

In Gen. 1:2 we read that during the creation the Spirit of God brooded over or hovered on the face of the waters. This was in imparting life in coöperation with the Creator Son. So also in the Economy of Re-

[23] In the preceding chapter mention is made of the passages which speak of Christ entering the Holy of Holies with His blood after His death. Evidently it was after His resurrection and with the Holy Spirit blood as the new and permanent life of His spiritual (pneumatikon) body. "Having therefore, brethren, boldness to enter into the holy place **by the blood of Jesus,** . . . a new and living way" (Heb. 10:19). "How much more shall the blood of Christ who through eternal Spirit offered Himself without blemish unto God" (9:14). Do we not enter into the Holy Place by the same Holy Spiritual blood that He did?

demption the Son is man's Re-creator along with the Holy Spirit's impartation by regeneration, and this followed by His Inhabitation unto the end of man's fellowship with the Father and fulfilment in His Sovereignty.

In the Incarnation Christ entered upon the personal sacrifice preparatory to that of Redemption in which He became the sacrifice of self-impartation. The open wounds of His crucifixion would not have remained in His risen body without definite purpose. Receive it who can, they are today the outlets of His infinite redeeming life for those who receive Him. Here the Holy Spirit as His life-blood is well adapted to such transfusion. In II Cor. 3:17 Paul identifies in the closest degree Christ and the Holy Spirit: "Now the Lord is the Spirit: and where the Spirit of the Lord is, there is liberty." And in the great Resurrection chapter (I Cor. 15:45) Paul also says: "The last Adam became a life-giving (a quickening) spirit."

After the Resurrection when the blood of Christ is mentioned, surely it is the blood of His resurrection body, which is the Holy Spirit. This means of the life in His risen body functions in Redemption's transfusion, re-creation and regeneration. It is also the blood which cleanses the Christian daily from sin. As previously cited more than once, I John 1:7 in using the verb *katherizei* in the present historical tense means, "keeps on cleansing from all sin." This could not be by the very blood of the body that died on the cross. It must refer to the new blood-life of the Holy Spirit in His resurrection body. Might not this be the "new and living way" of 10:19? However, if the physical blood had not been shed, Christ would not have died, and there would not then have been the spiritual blood of the resurrection body replacing it to be poured out from the open wounds of our risen and redeeming Saviour. Thus the cleansing, life-giving blood of the Risen Redeemer is metonymy for the Holy Spirit imparting Christ to cleanse from or obliterate sin. As we have seen, the Holy Spirit took up the life-function in the risen Body of the Lord, thus serving as its breath and blood.

The ministry of the Holy Spirit in the mediation of Redemption is a very great subject. In I Cor. 12:4 His work for and with Christ is presented:

> "Now there are diversities of gifts, but the same Spirit. And there are diversities of ministrations, and the same Lord. And there are diversities of workings, but the same God, who worketh all things in all. But to each one is given the manifestation of the Spirit to profit withal. . . . But all these worketh the one and the same Spirit, dividing to each one severally as He will."

If thus the Holy Spirit is indispensable in ministering in this most personal way, imparting these individual gifts to all who are Christ's, how equally essential must the Spirit of God be in Christ's Person for imparting the greatest gift of all, that of Christ Himself, His re-creating and cleansing life in Redemption? His vicarious sacrifice of His poured-out life fits us by its impartation to be heirs of God and joint-heirs with Him. In Rom. 8:10 we read, "The Spirit is life because of righteousness." This is the righteousness of Christ for us and in us.

Chapter Nine

CURRENT INTERPRETATIONS OF THE CROSS

Introduction

The Word of God is most admirable among books. Its purpose, however, is not reached by eliciting mere praise. It is a book of Divine utility and fidelity. But a small part of its usefulness becomes effective in even the greatest of its earthly admirers. There is a price we must pay to possess its best treasures for life-enrichment. In this it is like the Kingdom of Heaven; that is, it "suffers violence." Translated, this means, it requires aggressive earnestness. The more diligent we are in digging up its treasures, and the more inspired by the Spirit who wrote it, the saner our study and the greater our gain. But the profit does not end with ourselves. Its enrichment is greatest when turned into the currency of the Christian life. This is not meant to jingle like coins in our mental pockets; but instead to be passed on for investment in the lives about us.

1. The various books of the Bible have what corresponds to individuality in persons. The Psalms, Isaiah's foregleams of the Messiah, John's counterpart to this

in the history of the Only-Begotten Deity come in the flesh, like all the rest of the Scriptures have their distinctive features. It is the practical that prevails in them. This is a distinct fruit of the Holy Spirit. In this matter the Epistle to the Hebrews is as unique as any other book in the Bible. All the way through, the marks of the Spirit of God are upon it. Not least among evidences of the Spirit is this—his instrument neglected to add his name. But he succeeded in setting forth the New Covenant as the central doctrine of the New Testament writings.

I. Redemption From the Powers of Evil

Many are the great boulders of truth jutting out here and there all along the way which the Epistle to the Hebrews takes. One of these not far from the beginning has an importance all its own. The fragmentary character is in our treatment of it, and not in the truth it reveals. This is our Lord's *Redemption of man from the Powers of Evil.*

1. Hebrews 2:14 says: "Since the children are sharers in blood and flesh (the Greek order), He also Himself in like manner partook of the same; that through death He might bring to naught him that had the power of death, that is, the devil; and might deliver all them who through fear of death were all their lifetime subject to bondage."

We have noted that God's wrath is always aroused by the presence of sin; and that sin exists nowhere but in personality. The human, however, is not the only order of persons infested by sin. Angels fell by it.

They are an unmeasured territory of evil. Their numbers we do not know; but we do know the Word of God is as reliable about their existence as it is in other revelations. Human experience has corroborated the fact that their malign presence is with us. Divine Redemption has not ignored the need of mastery over the evil spirits. Our Lord has solved this along with all the rest of the problem of evil. He met the arch tempter after His baptism and fully vanquished his temptations. So Satan left Him for a season. He also cast out the demons from those possessed by them. As the time for the crucifixion drew nigh, Jesus said: "The Prince of this world cometh and hath nothing in me." But he did find some chaff in Peter. In Judas, the diabolus from the beginning, Satan found an ally, and hurried him on to perdition.

In His own death Jesus was not on the defensive. True, He was letting evil have for the time its way; but that was really a triumphant strategy of the most important offensive and victory over sin, evil and the devil. His Father had planned that decisive move in the campaign against sin. Then it was that Christ "led captivity captive." Thus He became Deliverer of all who sought His power in this great conflict. Though He died, that itself brought into action the very forces of the unity of the Trinity to overwhelm the disintegrating power of evil. He thus became God's dynamite to blast sin out of existence wherever His sacrificial presence came; and the impartation of Himself securing the inhabitation of the Holy Spirit left no human territory belonging to Him in the hands of the devil.

So at death He took the repentant robber with Him to Paradise and far beyond the reach of devil, demon, or sin. Yet some say He died a spiritual death.

In the passage quoted from the second chapter of Hebrews it is shown that Satan has power to put to death spiritually, as he did Adam and Eve. Sin is the great instrument of this death. Jesus delivers not only from both evil spirits and sin, but also from the fear of death.

2. From the first the Scriptures set forth the evil and power Satan and his hosts have. I Sam. 16:14 is an instance of this evil influence: "Now the Spirit of Jehovah departed from Saul, and an evil spirit from Jehovah troubled him." The Hebrew word is *bawath,* and means affrighted or terrified. Later this spirit is more at home in him. In 18:10 we read: "And it came to pass that on the morrow (after a fit of angry jealousy of David), that an evil spirit from God came mightily upon Saul, and he prophesied in the midst of the house." The Revised Version says "raved." The usual word, "*naba,*" is used, meaning "prophecy," but here in the hithpael it does mean to rave. What are we to make of this statement that the evil spirit was from God?

Some help may be obtained by taking into account the regular Hebrew way of conceiving and representing the *immediacy* of God in everything which came to pass. There were no secondary causes in their cosmology. When the wind blew, that was God's wrath. When the lightning flashed, there God flamed forth.

Not only are evil spirits from God, but He sets them at work. I Kings 22:20 represents Jehovah as calling for a volunteer from "all the host of heaven standing by Him on His right hand and on His left." He wants a lying spirit to go forth and be in the mouth of Ahab's prophets to entice him to his death by taking their advice in war. This is dramatic to the limit.

The first chapter of Job similarly represents Satan as coming before God and challenging the reality and integrity of Job's faith in God. He admits that he can do nothing to prove that Job is paid by God to be good, unless he is permitted. He is tethered by God, though the tether is not so very short. So long as the evil spirits keep within the bounds of God's permission, they may go forth *as from Jehovah,* though as a rule they do not at all represent Him in grace, but in judgment. They are never pleasing in His sight. The New Testament note is stronger. I John 3:8 says our Lord was "manifested that He might destroy the works of the devil."

II. Conflicting Views Offer Conflicting Interpretations

The more conflicting the theories of Redemption, the more conflicting their corresponding interpretations of the Scriptures with which they deal. It is strange that the more important any matter set forth in the Word of God, the more certain the divergence of human opinions about it. Hence it could not be otherwise than that there is decided conflict over the method and measures God has taken to meet the evil of sin and to solve its problem. The twenty centuries of Christianity have seen very many and varied views on this most important matter of Redemption.

1. As to the conflict over the interpretation of the biblical teaching on this matter, it is evident that the mind of man needs to be Divinely steadied and illumined when studying the utter madness of the world's deepest insanity in sin, and the wisdom of God in what He has done about it. Surely we could do nothing at all in properly interpreting God's way with it, had He not patiently given us the whole Bible story about this battlefield, how the conflict began, how it has raged through the centuries, and now seems to be nearing its final stage.

2. Sometimes the human mind is rather easily warped in Scripture interpretation by the theory it offers in explanation of Redemption. Some prefer the prophetic material, and the further back the better. For this reason some put prophecy ahead of actual Gospel history and teaching in explaining Redemption. They should remember that prophecy is prophecy and not history. The writer not long ago listened to the head of an important school of the prophets while he was a guest preacher in the City of Brotherly Love. He took his text in the Messianic Psalm which opens, "My God, my God, why hast thou forsaken me?" He began with the declaration that prophecy gives us a clearer and more helpful account as to what really happened in the death of Christ, than can be found in the historical accounts of the New Testament. Evidently that seemed

perfectly true to a specialist in prophecy. His conclusions, therefore, were sheer relativity; just as any mother views her own babe as the latest and the last in baby-beauty. It is easier to forgive her bias than to excuse that of a teacher of preachers who handles the Word of God in the pulpit in sorry self-deception.

3. To impartial judgment, when prophecy has passed into history, history has more light to shed on prophecy than prophecy has to give to accomplished history. Be that as it may, and taking the specialist on his own chosen ground, the twenty-second Psalm does not teach the Father's literal forsaking of the Son on the cross. No Messianic psalm can picture the Saviour as more alive to God than does this very one. If actually He were forsaken, He could not be so perfectly responsive.

In the first place, psalms are not written to celebrate the plight of spiritual destitution in being utterly forsaken of God. What could be more inappropriate? When spiritually forsaken or estranged no one writes a hymn about his experience. This whole psalm is anything else than a hymn of being deserted by God. Its conflict is not with God the Father deserting God the Son.

Evidently the inspired person who penned the psalm did not intend to have his very first words in it taken literally, since all the rest of it would contradict them explicitly. Never did a psalm picture a soul more alive in God and yearning for Him. Manifestly the writer could not have meant actual abandonment by God, when in this hymn he praises God for His faithfulness, and twice says: "Be not far from me!" (Verses

11, 19). In the twenty-sixth verse he goes on to say, "They shall praise Jehovah, that seek after Him." Throughout the whole hymn it pictures the Messiah as doing both—praising God and seeking after Him. It is a crime to tear away the first verse from all the rest.

If this Messianic psalm was fulfilled in Christ's experience on the cross, there is not a hint in it that He was to be actually abandoned by the Father who has never deserted any soul that trusted in Him. Even taking the circumstances of the psalm as all about Christ's experience on the cross, the Messiah is pictured as being surrounded by scorning, bitter, murderous enemies. This is the situation which gives the true setting to the opening words, "My God, my God, why hast thou left me to the mercy of those whose wicked will it is to destroy me?" This psalmist did not prophesy that the Son of God was to become a lost soul while dying to save the lost.

III. The Story of the Witnesses of Christ's Death

The Scriptures can be made to teach almost anything one wishes, if single passages be plucked completely out of the whole context story. It is true that the eyewitnesses of Christ's death heard Him quote these words from the twenty-second Psalm, "My God, my God, why hast thou forsaken me?" What did our Lord mean by them? The other things He said surely serve to show this. Within a very few minutes later He said, "It is finished." "Father, into thy hands I commend (or commit) my spirit." Matthew says, "He dismissed His spirit." *Aphēken,* He sent away (Matt. 27:50). John 19:30,

"He gave up His spirit." *Paredōken,* delivered up. Being Divine, He must take part in active participation in His own death and the committing of Himself to God. No one Person of the Trinity ever does anything which is not shared in coöperation by the other two. Even in the death of the Son's body this was true. He said, "I have power to lay down my life, and I have power to take it again."

1. There are the seven recorded utterances of Christ on the cross. Six of these show no sense of Divine abandonment. He could not have committed Himself in death to a God and Father whom He believed had forsaken Him. If spiritually dead His faith in Him would be gone. There was the brief word in tender love committing His mother to the care of John. Next came the pathetic, "I thirst." The loss of His precious blood would account for that. The prayer of the repentant robber was answered by, "Verily I say unto thee, today shalt thou be with me in Paradise." Doubtless the first of all His words on the cross were, "Father, forgive them; for they know not what they do." If these sayings on the cross mean anything, surely it is, through all His suffering and death He remained in unbroken fellowship with the Father. Both before and after quoting the first verse of the twenty-second Psalm, He remained the same blessed Jesus, thoughtful of others, forgiving His murderers, and saving a poor sinner dying beside Him. Though suffering in intense and immense strain till His heart broke, He remained in unfailing unity of unbroken fellowship with the Father.

According to John 19:30, as just noted, Jesus said: "It is finished: and He bowed His head, and gave up His spirit." Some think that Christ was under hallucination due to mortal agony when He uttered this historic cry. But He had refused the stupefying potion that He might be free from all deadening and delusion. His mind was never more clear and reliable.

2. But there was a necessary Divine forsaking in His death. *It was properly a physical forsaking.* In any physical death God must be more than spectator. Jesus Himself said: "Not a sparrow falls to the ground without your heavenly Father." This does not mean, without your Heavenly Father knowing it, as so many read it. Jesus was so sensitive to God in every movement, He discerned the Father's acts where ordinary men saw nothing Divine at all. When the Father's movement was within the Son Himself, how much more must the Son be aware of it.

There is good evidence that the strain under which our Lord was suffering had reached the limit of His heart's power of endurance. II Cor. 13:4 says, "For He was crucified through weakness." This refers to the limitation of His mortal body. The flesh was not omnipotent. No doubt He could have withstood the effect of the crucifixion much longer, had not His soul suffering become the immediate cause of His death. In His Incarnate Person He was realizing the biting bitterness, the godless inhumanity that was seeking to expel Him from this world, to undo the Incarnation. The same perfect and wondrous soul so sensitive to

God was equally sensitive to the character of the atrocious enmity of iniquity. Phil. 2:8 says, "And being found in fashion as a man, He humbled Himself, becoming *obedient unto death,* yea, the death of the cross." That infinite obedience to the Father passed the bounds of His body's endurance. This drew forth the agonizing "Why?" for He was being faithful and true to the limit. He was "faithful even unto death." His self-realization was in loyal subservience to the Father's will, and by which He fulfilled Himself.

3. There was difficulty for the Father as well as for the Son. When that great human-Divine heart broke under the strain, the Father could no longer sustain life contrary to the way He had ordained for it in heart-beats and blood-circulation. The Word of God had said, "Cursed is every one that hangeth on a tree." He could not bless with His physically sustaining presence this unnatural, inhuman, and ungodly order of death. He was not dying even a martyr's death, such as Stephen did. In this sense Christ by being put to death by crucifixion became a curse for us, as Gal. 3:13 and Deut. 21:23 set forth. Sinners put the curse of that accursed death upon the Christ. Jesus' death was like His birth as being without a parallel.

The Son of God must have felt more keenly than we are able to measure, the withdrawal of the Father from the life of His body. God the Father had dwelt in that blessed body from its beginning in the Virgin's womb. How it must have pained the Father to depart from that broken heart which had beaten more true to Him than any other. But He could no longer dwell in the best heart He had ever inhabited. He had to forsake it. That was the compulsion of the consistency of His Divine nature, constitutional relation and place.

For the first time as far as we know, He Who had taken the place of a bond-slave in obedient death at the hand of sin, called Him God instead of Father, though He Himself was God as truly as was the Father. Even as God to the Incarnate One the Father was vastly more to Him than He had ever been to any man. There is a word for agony the cross has given to us. It is "excruciating" (*ex cruce*). Though Jesus had been bearing that excruciating agony of His physical sufferings on the cross, He was spiritually sustained by the Father and the Holy Spirit also till that break in the heart physically central in his bodily life. Spiritually the weight of the world's sin was upon Him, for He had undertaken the Divine problem of solving in Person human redemption from it. Perhaps the unspeakably bitter part of His agony was the bearing of what seemed to be the hindering of the hand of God by sin, in letting Him suffer on, yea, even in a way compelling a sort of coöperation with iniquity. There had often been that mystery of iniquity, for example in adultery, which often forced the hand of God to coöperate in producing a life, a child of shame, a human personality. This no doubt David felt when in his awakening he said, "Against Thee, even (or specially) Thee, have I sinned and done this evil in Thy sight." Is there not an utterly abnormal limitation of the hand of God by sin? No wonder then that there reappears in the crucifixion also "The Mystery of Iniquity."

That was the last agony when the Father in fidelity to His nature, constitutional relation and place as God was compelled to withdraw from the broken physical life of the Son. Such a Divinely sensitive soul as that of the Christ had suffered the bitter agony of immediate contact with the work and nature of sin till the strain of it broke His physical endurance. Only God the Father and the Son Himself along with the infinitely sensitive Holy Spirit could feel, know and realize fully the pain of the plight the Saviour's dying sacrifice entailed. The blessed Triune Godhead would not be such unless the Father and the Holy Spirit suffered with the Saviour and felt what He felt. When the last sacrificial wrench came, His physical life could last no longer, and His soul was thus expelled from His body and from this world. What an unparalleled Divine experience was there! Never before was it uttered, and never again will the cry of the crucified Son be heard, "My God, My God, why hast Thou forsaken Me?" It really meant that the Son was sacrificing Himself and not the essential Unity of the Trinity.

IV. Counterpart Passages of Mutual Explanation

There is real regard for the Scriptures and as real help in noting how frequently the Holy Spirit gives us counterpart statements instead of the partial, and often these in proximity to each other. The Word of God is anything but one-sided. The complementary views it presents are often the divine and the human sides in turn. For example, in Exodus chapters 7 to 14 some fifteen times it is said either that God hardened Pharaoh's heart, or that Pharaoh hardened his own heart. There cannot help being God's part in either the hardening or the softening of the heart. God is not a half God with part place in providential relation. He must ever control the evil as well as direct the good. *To represent either side alone would not be the whole truth.* And a half truth is often more dangerous than an outright lie. Some build their theories on the passages on but one side to the exclusion of the other. No wonder that one-sided and perverse theories result.

1. Perhaps there is no passage about Christ's death more frequently quoted from the Old Testament than Isa. 53:6, "Jehovah hath laid on Him the iniquity of us all." The Hebrew expression is, "caused to meet on Him." This precious passage expresses the same truth as many other scriptures do about the Divine Program and Appointment in the sacrifice of Christ. That is very necessary truth as to God's part in planning and carrying through this greatest of all matters ever enacted on earth or in all the ages. But does anyone ever remember hearing coupled with it the counterpart passage in the same paragraph? Two verses before this (verse 4) there had been said, "Yet we did esteem Him smitten of God and afflicted." The Hebrew word translated "esteem" is *chashab,* which means imagine, suppose, count, consider, impute, invent, regard, think. This is what those ever since

looking only on the Divine side have supposed, invented, thought, imagined, namely, that it was really God who smote and afflicted the Christ on the cross. The other side of the truth is that it was sin's job to do that, not God's at all. Ungodly sinners smote and crucified Him. The unrighteous, murderous, plotting professors of religion could be depended upon to serve as the devil's agents in the crucifixion-murder of Christ. It was part of God's plan to let them have their way in this, and thus outwit sin.

The verse before this (verse 3) is on the same line: "He was despised and rejected (forsaken, destitute—Heb. *chadel*) of men; a man of sorrows, and acquainted with grief (other's sickness); and as one from whom men hide their face He was despised; *and we esteemed Him not* (*Chashab* again)." It is in view of all this that the divine side is given. "Like sheep we have gone astray. We have turned every one to his own way; and Jehovah hath caused to meet on Him the iniquity of us all," like the picture of birds coming from every quarter settling on a tree.

The same program of presenting *both sides* goes on again from verses 7 to 9 inclusive; then the Divine side again: "He was cut off out of the land of the living for the transgression of my people to whom the stroke was due, (or, was He stricken). And they (certainly not God) made His grave with the wicked and with a rich man in His death." Then turning back again to the Divine part, "Yet it pleased the Lord (Jehovah) to bruise Him; He hath put Him to grief; when thou shalt make His soul (or, when His soul shall make) a *trespass-offering for sin, and the pleasure of Jehovah shall prosper in His hand.* (Carefully note!) He shall see of the travail of His soul, and shall be satisfied." (No spiritual death there.) Here we have the third side, that of the Redeemer Himself. He justifies many because He shall bear their iniquities. He poured out His soul unto death and was numbered with the transgressors (the two robbers).

When the Spirit of God has His way, both the human and the Divine aspects including that of Christ, are fairly presented. For example, the Pentecostal account (Acts 2:23), *which is history and not prophecy,* states it this way: "Him being delivered up by the determinate counsel and foreknowledge of God, ye by the hands of lawless men (men without the law, the Roman soldiers) did crucify and slay." This passage gives faithfully both the Divine and the human sides, namely, how the wise hand of God and the unholy hands of sinners wrought in this same all-important matter of the world's Redemption. Unless God had actually permitted it, sin could not have done it. In it God was no less God in love and absolute righteousness, and sin was none the less sin in ungodly, murderous hate.

2. II Cor. 5:21 deals with the same matter: "Him Who knew no sin, He made to be sin on our behalf (*huper* not *anti*); that we might become the righteousness of God in Him." *It is unmistakable that Christ was sinned against.* By its effect sin made Him *sin in effect,* a sin-slain personality. Only by permitting

sin to do this could God be said to have made Him sin. Never as cause can anyone be made sin. But upon any and all of us might fall the *effect* of sin, if only by inheritance or heredity. Only we ourselves can make ourselves sin in cause. Upon the Christ "Who did no sin," the murderous effect of sin fell. But even that, too, He must permit. Let us repeat again: John 10:17, 18 says, "Therefore doth the Father love me, because I lay down my life, that I may take it again. No one taketh it away from me, but I lay it down of myself. I have power to lay it down, and I have power to take it again. *This commandment received I from my Father*." And the Father Himself could easily have prevented this sin, had he not planned the defeat of it and of all sin by letting this sin have its way in putting the Son to death, and by the crucifixion effect upon the Person of the Redeemer which opened the infinite outflow of what we may call the spiritual blood of Christ's risen body to blot out sin, and thus make us "the righteousness of God in Him." This "made" righteousness is at least the absence of sin by cleansing from it.

3. On this passage (II Cor. 5: 21) Beyschlag has the following comment:

> "The idea of making amends for, of blotting out, our sins before God, in order that we might be acquitted of them, or justified, that is the idea of atonement, is really present here though the word is not. But we do not find here, for all that the idea of an atonement by substitutionary suffering of the punishment of sin—a conception which is not expressed in Paul either here or anywhere else. . . . But, what is more, the passage shows positive traces that the exchange between

Christ and us which the apostle has in view cannot be thought of in the form of the abstract juridical doctrine of substitution. We find such traces in the fact that it does not read *anti hemon* but *huper hemon*, and that *en auto* is added to the second half of the verse."[24]

In the fifteenth, a few verses previous, we read: "that one died for all, therefore all died; and He died for all that they that live should no longer live unto themselves, but unto Him Who for their sakes (*huper* again) died and rose again." Here the object of the Redeemer's death is stated to be unselfish, sacrificial living unto Him. An interesting comparison of views is here noticed by Beyschlag:

"That is a statement which sets forth with unsurpassable clearness the profound distinction between the Anselmic and the Pauline view of the saving significance of the death of Jesus. According to Anselm it ought to read: He died, one instead of all, so that they need not all die, *viz.* the eternal death of condemnation. But Paul says: He died, one for the advantage of all, and therefore they all died (in Him); they inwardly mortified their natural wickedness, and died to sin. Only the utmost violence could interpret this Pauline statement into Anselm's meaning: 'No one now dies because of his sins, since the death of Christ is valid as the death of all.' "[25]

V. Did Christ Die a Spiritual Death?

Some endeavor to put penalty at the heart of Redemption, and represent that penalty as spiritual death. They certainly could not have Christ bear more severe penalty than to die spiritually. Nor could they imagine a death more out of keeping with what it is supposed to accomplish, namely, to take away sin.

[24] **New Testament Theology,** Vol. 2, pp. 152, 153.
[25] **New Testament Theology,** Vol. 2, p. 141.

1. Perhaps first of all we should define spiritual death. Manifestly it is dying to God, to all normal relationship to, and activity in, Him. It is necessarily the cessation of life in God. For Jesus to die spiritually would be to die in spirit. By this death He would cease to have faith in the Father. He could then no longer love and obey Him, no longer be filled with and led by the Holy Spirit. He would also necessarily cease carrying out the holy Divine purposes for which He was offering up Himself to God. In a word, by dying spiritually He would renounce His place in the Trinity, that is, die to His Deity. He could not die spiritually and remain the Holy Son of God. Spiritual death is spiritual dying to all the life He had in the Spirit. It could not be less than that and be spiritual death at all. Satan is dead to God. To propose that Christ should become as the devil is, in order to redeem from sin and from the devil, would be surely agreeable to Satan, to say the least.

One must surely see that if for Satan there is no way back to life in God, there would also be no way back for Christ. Spiritual death would mean even more for Him, for there was infinitely more of Him to die. As He is an infinite and eternal Person, His spiritual death would be infinite and eternal. With the Godhead thus broken up, with death having entered it, its unity and spiritual life would be gone forever.

2. Is the spiritual death of the Son of God possible? Ten thousand times, No! If "God cannot lie," in the same way and for the same reason the Son of God cannot spiritually die. For Christ to die to the Father

and the Holy Spirit would equally involve their death to Him. In the unity of the Godhead how could they be alive to Him and He dead to them? Surely this substitutionary spiritual death-penalty is to propose entirely too much—even the annihilation of the whole triune Godhead.

If for Christ to die spiritually is impossible, it is little use to consider what would take place if He died spiritually, except to show its repulsive unreasonableness. Surely a dead Person of the Godhead is the very greatest contradiction possible in terms. If Christ had died spiritually, this would finally proclaim that He never was Deity. His Incarnation did not change His nature as essentially God the Son. Theologically, it is impossible to defend the view that it is possible for a Person of the Triune Godhead to die spiritually. This we may see as we state what the Trinity is, namely, a triunity of three interexistent, counterpart, correlate Other-Selves who in sacrificial other-consciousness live for each other absolutely. Since the Godhead consists in this transcendent order of three Interpersonalities, interconscious and completely inseparable in fellowship and indestructible in unity, we may infer that the special assault of sin upon it by means of the crucifixion of the Son could not possibly result in its disruption. God would not have undertaken this sacrifice of Redemption by means of the death on the cross, if the unity of the Trinity and the Person of the Son were not able to endure or withstand it.

3. The murder of the Incarnate Son could not go beyond His physical death, for He proved to be an

invincible stronghold against all the effect which demon, man and sin could bring to bear upon Him. Then, too, underneath, within, and all about Him was the final strategic stronghold against iniquity, the Absolute Unity of the Trinity. In no way and in no place was God found wanting when the death of the Incarnate One came to pass. Sin's power in effect of disunity is very great; but its power of disintegration is not infinite as is the indestructible unity of the Trinity. That unassailable, inseparable, irresistible, invulnerable and invincible interrelation of the Persons of the Godhead is the ultimate in Divine Security, even as in ultimate character and disposition there is the absolute Holiness of God in unapproachable essence, uncreated existence, and infinite perfection.

4. Escape from these conclusions is sought by saying, it was but a temporary spiritual death which Jesus suffered. *Where in the Scriptures is this taught?* Human persons may be under spiritual death temporarily, because there is the power of Christ to redeem them. But when the Redeemer Himself is thought to be spiritually dead, there can be no super-redeemer to redeem Him. Christ Himself rose from the dead and was the power of spiritual resurrection to all who come by faith unto Him; but there would be no hope, were Christ Himself dead to all life in God, for then *Hope itself* were dead, and all spiritual resurrection also would be impossible.

Still others say, Christ needed to remain spiritually dead only as long as those to be redeemed had been spiritually dead, and that God by decree could impose spiritual death and withdraw it as soon as it pleased Him. But God never imposes spiritual death. That is solely the work and result of sin. God is *the God of life,* not of spiritual death. Moreover, no fiat of God could transfer spiritual death to a Person of the Godhead. Christ bore sin in effect, in result, not by fiat, but in being *sinned against;* and *spiritual death has never once come or resulted by being sinned against.* Christ did not die within Himself by sin as cause at work there, because *it never got there,* for the Word of God bears witness that "He was without sin," "That He did no sin."

Spiritual death is not something so easily visited on or withdrawn from the Author of Life in such a way as to flash in and then as quickly out and disappear. It is not like light at all, but rather like the blackness of darkness indescribable. Since the Scriptures tell us that "in Him all things consist," that is, *hold together,* then the very universe must have flashed out of existence and then in again with Christ's temporary spiritual death. Once more, may we ask, *Do the Scriptures teach this?* Is not this program of spiritual death for the Redeemer unto spiritual life an addition to the Word of God neither in kind nor in keeping with it? To what lengths people do go to save a theory of infinite difficulty and darkness, when they make incompatible additions to Scripture teaching, and would break up the very Godhead to corroborate them!

VI. Did Christ Die the Death We Deserve?

This is practically the same thing over again, viz., spiritual death. Clearly the death we deserved and received was spiritual. What is emphasized is the supposed *quid pro quo,* the equivalent that Christ suffered for us in penalty. The question naturally arises, if we have already suffered this spiritual death, why does God in the name of righteousness call for Jesus Christ to suffer it over again? Even if penalty be the main thing, why exact it twice? And what sort of forgiveness is it that first must pour out the penalty of spiritual death on some one else?

1. Spiritual death is entire helplessness for good spiritually, and does not become one whit more possible to the Son of God because it is described as that which we deserved. Then for Christ to suffer a spiritual death is not an equivalent in any way. We may die to God as one of His creatures. Christ would die as the Creator-Son of God in the Godhead. He is vastly more important, in His existence as God and Creator, than all the whole race of mankind. In any case penalty is always earned, is the automatic effect of sin.

As we have clearly seen in the Epistle to the Hebrews and other scriptures, Christ offered up Himself an acceptable sacrifice because His blood, His sacrificial life, His sin-destroying spirit and power is that which God desired as effective in putting away sin. Then the other half of His Redemption is His power of self-impartation, re-creation, and the bringing in the inhabitation of the Holy Spirit. Now a spiritual death could be efficacious only in destroying both halves of the Covenant of Redemption, the offering and the bequeathment.

2. A spiritual death, or a spiritually dead Christ, could not possibly be an acceptable offering to the God of Life Eternal, and He could not then be to Him a sacrifice at all, for that spiritually dead could not offer itself in sacrifice to God. Moreover, the spiritually dead Christ could impart only spiritual death, if thus He imparted anything. His power of re-creation would be gone, and also His ability to give the Holy Spirit. How also could the spiritually dead act as High Priest and at the same time be acceptable offering to God?

That the Saviour could not save from sin except He must first duplicate in Himself the spiritual effect of sin in spiritual death, is little like what we find in the Epistle to the Hebrews. There is not an atom of spiritual death ascribed in it to Jesus our Lord, nor a scintilla of penalty imposed by God upon Him. Either it is wrong and, to say the least, incomplete description, or this claim that Christ had to die our spiritual death to redeem us, is an invention of some other than Christ's spirit and other than by the Holy One who inspired the Scriptures. Would it not be a strange thing that what called for the greatest ability in every way is instead supposed to be secured by the very greatest disability and disaster? This theory of the necessity of His spiritual death to fit Christ with ability as Redeemer, runs counter to the spiritual law that things bring forth after their kind. Spiritual life for us could not possibly come from spiritual death in Christ. And it is as utterly impossible in all other kinds of equivalence; for example, in the supposed righteousness of demanding the spiritual death of Deity to cure the unrighteousness of the sin of humanity. That is not Redemption, but an uncured carnival of absolute impossibilities. Spiritual death is the greatest evil of which we know. What sort of reasoning is it which proposes that this greatest evil can be made right by duplicating the similar greatest evil in the Lord Jesus Christ? Did not God see enough spiritual death without adding to it that of His own beloved Son? Where does this claim come from, namely, that there can be satisfaction to God by spiritual death? That is not at all like the Father whom the Son revealed. That is not like the Holy Spirit we know who as perfect Divine sensitiveness abhors sin, let alone its final fruit in spiritual death. If God "takes no pleasure in the death of the wicked," how can He take pleasure in the spiritual death of His Son? No object, purpose, or aim could be to the Father what the Eternal Son is.

As already noted earlier, the words "penal" and "penalty" never occur in the Scriptures. If the Spiritual-Death-Penalty-Theory were the true interpretation of the Heart of Divine Redemption as set forth in the New Testament, then these words should have naturally been used all through the Scriptures. Either penalty is not fundamental to Redemption, or the Bible is thus most seriously defective. Evidently the manufacturers of this theory have more faith in penalty than God has, judging by the Word of God come to us and its message of redeeming love. Love never damns. Sin has that job all to itself. Love never inflicts spiritual death, for "Love never fails." The great object lesson of what spiritual death can do, is the fate of the fallen angels and the souls already lost hopelessly. All these will suffer to all eternity without an atom of good result to themselves. On this theory of Redemption by Penalty all the demons and lost human souls should become best redeemed of all.

The fact is, Christ is spiritual life in infinite fulness in God. Spiritual death cannot be added to such an infinite measure of spiritual life. *They do not add up.* And spiritual death inflicted on spiritual life could never enable it to become *a source of life.* Jesus on the Cross never died *in* spiritual death but *to it,* as all the scripture accounts show. As we have mentioned elsewhere, to demand the spiritual death of the Son would have been really to demand at the same time the same thing of the Father and of the Holy Spirit, for *They ever live in and by each other.* This theory of spiritual death in Christ personifies penalty as if God; yes, *it deifies penalty,* instead of the true view of Christ as the Incarnate Personalization of the Love of God in Jesus Christ our Redeeming Lord.

Forgotten by penalists may be the fact that the Father can do nothing to the Divine Son that He does not in great measure do to Himself. Unity in the Trinity if less than this would be its shadow and not its reality. While we have on earth no such extent and quality of unity as the Godhead, what we do to one another in large measure is what we do to ourselves.

Still others say that the Father after inflicting on the Son spiritual death, revived Him from it a little later on. But who revived the dead Father to enable

Him to do this? The Scriptures record the resurrection of Christ's body. Is the body of more importance than His spirit, since there is no account of that spiritual resurrection?

3. As this theory evidently takes no account of Christ's physical death, and makes spiritual death the substance of Redemption, why the Incarnation? But some would have even more than spiritual death. We have heard it preached as the Word of the Lord that as the Lord hung on the cross the Father not only smote Him with spiritual death, but also in the Divine anger poured out the vials of holy wrath upon Him; in righteous judgment of hot displeasure He pronounced Him accursed; in utter wrath with Him He turned His back upon Him; and because He was in the sinner's place, the Father forsook, abandoned, left Him to the bitterness of spiritual death. Do not the echoes of *what Jesus Himself said* come back again to us? We need to quote them often, they are so different from what certain theorists say. "Therefore doth the Father love me, because I lay down my life, that I may take it again. I have power to lay it down, and I have power (right) to take it again." Evidently the Son of God did not apprehend that He was to die spiritually, and that the Father would revile and forsake Him spiritually. The Epistle to the Hebrews reveals the heavenward side of what actually took place when the Great High Priest offered Himself without spot or blemish to God and as King of Peace and Righteousness was seated at the Father's right hand in glory. Was the King High Priest spiritually fit to offer Himself to God?

VII. Testimony of the Scriptures as to How Christ Died

The Word of God is anything but silent as to the kind of death that our Lord died. Of course, He suffered in soul and spirit as well as in body. That had a share in perfecting and fulfilling Him as our Redeemer and consumming our Redemption.

1. Our Saviour said: "On the third day I am perfected." In the Epistle to the Hebrews (5: 8, 9) we read, "Though He was a Son, yet learned *obedience* by the things which He suffered; *and having been made perfect,* He became unto all them that obey Him the Author (*aitios,* concrete cause) of eternal salvation." Here we have the personal point of view again. The Saviour by His death is *perfected* in Person by His infinite obedience. He is made perfect as the Perfect Cause of our salvation to all eternity. Everything centers in the Person of Christ, especially its power of becoming *perfected* as our Redeemer. In 12:2 He is "the author and finisher of our faith." A different word is here used for Author, *archēgos,* originating author, chief leader. Would to God that all had Him as the Originator of their faith, and then He surely would be the object of it as well. What He became by His death shows us the kind of death it was, not a spiritual death, but in that *obedience* which in Him became the foundation of our eternal salvation.

Heb. 2:9, "That He should taste death for every man." Spiritual death is infinitely too terrible to be called a "taste." 2:14, "He also Himself in like manner partook of the same (flesh and blood); that through death (*of flesh and blood*) He might bring to naught him that hath the power of death." 10:10, "We have been sanctified through the offering of the body of Jesus Christ once for all" Spiritual death would not be offering anything, certainly not the offering of His body once for all. 10:12, "He offered up one sacrifice (that of His body) for sins for ever. . . . There remaineth no more sacrifice for sins."

2. I Peter 3:18, "Being put to death in the flesh, but made alive in the spirit." Evidently Peter had never heard of or believed in Christ's spiritual death. I Peter 2:24, "Who His own self bare our sins in His body upon the tree, that we having died unto sins, might live unto righteousness." This passage also makes its own clear contribution as to the kind of death Christ died. Phil. 2:8, "Becoming obedient even unto death, yea, the death of the cross." This, too, was not a spiritual death. Col. 1:22, "Yet now hath He reconciled in the body of His flesh through death." That is His physical death, the only kind the Apostle ever heard of. Rom. 6:10, "For the death that He died (the physical), He died unto sin once for all." The context shows Paul meant the death of Christ's body. "Once for all" shows that there was no other; absolutely the only death; for a spiritual death in the Son of God was just as impossible as the death of God Himself.

3. In closing this chapter we may note the correspondence between the character of Christ's death and

the character of His ministry that followed it. Surely a spiritual death would be the opposite to any fit preparation for the ministry of reconciliation and of redemption. Instead, He passed obediently through the physical death the Father had commanded, and to His appointed post-death ministry of imparting to sinners Himself as the means of sin-cleansing and sin-mastering life. So the vicarious death He died fulfilling absolutely the nature of God in relation to man and sin, and His perfect obedience to the Father submitting to the physical death sin inflicted, offering Himself by the eternal, sacrificial spirit of the Godhead, perfectly prepared Him as a riven, crucified and risen Person with open and unhealed wounds to pour out to lost humanity the blood of His Redemption. "Having obtained eternal redemption . . . How much more shall the blood of Christ who through (no, the) eternal spirit offered Himself without blemish unto God, cleanse your conscience from dead works to serve the living God? And for this cause He is the Mediator of a new Covenant (*diathēkē*, a will-covenant, a bequeathment-agreement)" (Heb. 9:12 ff). "Now, once at the end of the ages hath He been manifested to put away sin (*eis athetēsin*, unto complete extermination) by the sacrifice of Himself" (9:26 ff). Surely a spiritual death could never lead to or prepare for such an eternal and infinite Divine Sacrifice in Person!

CHAPTER TEN

THE NEW CREATION BY THE NEW COVENANT

INTRODUCTION

THERE are at least three great complementary phases of Christ's redemptive impartation in the fulfilment of His bequeathment in the New Covenant. These are—*The New Creation, the New Relation, and the New Inhabitation.* They will be considered in this and the two following chapters. In this one there will be discussed the New Creation in three prominent phases—*the New Person, the New Nature,* and *the New Life.* Together these have long been known under the name of *Regeneration.* Under these three heads we shall proceed to consider it.

1. We have already said that Christ in Divine offices is Revealer, Creator and Sacrifice in Person. True to the first part of the New Covenant, He revealed the Father, "He that hath seen me, hath seen the Father," and the Holy Spirit, "I will send you another Paraclete" (Comforter), and also Himself, "I am the way, the truth, and the life." He has ever been the Father's Agent in creation. For the New Creation He dedicated Himself in the New Bequeathment as our New Creator.

This means the ruin and havoc caused by sin in us He undertook not only to end, but also to repair and to improve on the first creation. Being Divine Sacrifice in Person, the main thing He does in re-creation is to build Himself into human personalities, making them "Sons in Christ Jesus." In this task He reproduces sacrificial personality in us.

I. The New Person in Christ Jesus

There is the Great Problem in this task of Re-Creation which we should consider first. It would have been far easier for the Creator to bring into being entirely new persons. But that would not be redeeming already existing sinners by His regeneration. The great problem arising in this is *to preserve our personal identity*, while making us really new persons in Him. God is always the great respecter of the integrity of personality. Hence in this new creation He must leave intact that essential to perpetuating our identity in personality, despite the fact that what is left of the old is full of selfishness, treachery and decay caused by iniquity.

Necessarily, then, so-called Christian personality is not all Christian or regenerate. This Paul has discussed in Romans and elsewhere. He carefully distinguished between the old nature and the new, between that of "the flesh" and that "in the Spirit." In 7:18 ff. he says, "For I know that in me, that is, in my flesh, dwelleth no good thing. . . . (22) For I delight in the law of God after the inward man; but I see a different law in my members, warring against the law of my mind. . . . (24) Wretched man that I am! who shall deliver me out of this body of death?"

1. That the flesh and body of death is not merely physical nature, is evident from the spiritual nature of some of its fruits. In Gal. 5:16 ff. Paul shows the contrast between the two natures: "Walk by the Spirit, and ye shall not fulfil the lust of the flesh. For the flesh things plainly not physical: idolatry, sorcery, the flesh; for these are contrary the one to the other." Then he goes on to enumerate among the works of the flesh things plainly not physical: idolatry, sorcery, enmities, strife, jealousies, wraths, factions, divisions, heresies, envyings.

In II Cor. 5:17, "Wherefore if any man is in Christ, he is a new creature," better—"there is a new creation." Gal. 6:15 says, "For neither is circumcision anything, nor uncircumcision, but a new creature" (creation). And Eph. 4:22, 24, "Put away, as concerning your manner of life, the old man, that waxeth corrupt after the lust of deceit; and that ye be renewed in the spirit of your mind; and put on the new man, that is after God created in righteousness and holiness of truth." This agrees with what is said about Christ as Creator. Col. 1:14 ff., "The Son of His love in whom we have our redemption, the forgiveness of our sins; who is the image of the invisible God, the firstborn of all creation; for in Him were all things created, in the heavens and upon the earth, things visible and things invisible, whether thrones or dominions or principalities or powers; all things have been created through Him, and unto Him; and He is before all things, and in Him all things hold together."

2. In what part of us does personality arise or center? Certainly not in the body, nor in the soul, which is mainly the life of the body. Then it must be *in the spirit.* This, as before said, is the part that distinguishes us from mere animals. It is our capacity for God. By sin we lose right regard for and affinity with God. This is where the new creation takes place—in the spirit. "Create in me a clean heart, O God; and renew a right spirit within me." Some may object to this Old Testament prayer; but David knew something worth while about re-creation and renewal in God. Perhaps some New Testament passages may apply more closely. Eph. 2:13 ff., "But now in Christ Jesus ye that once were far off, are made nigh by the blood of Christ. . . . That He might create in Himself of the two (Jew and Gentile) one new man." Verse 10, "For we are His workmanship, created in Christ Jesus for good works." Col. 3:9 ff., "Seeing ye have put off the old man with his doings, and have put on the new man, that is being renewed unto knowledge after the image of Him that created him." Rev. 4:11, "Worthy art Thou, our Lord and our God, to receive the glory and the honor and the power: for Thou didst create all things, and because of Thy will they were, and were created."

3. Such passages all concern the fact of the New Creation by or in Christ Jesus. But they do not say when and how and where the new personality in Him

arises. Perhaps the historical incident of the ninth chapter of John may be of help. As to the man born blind, our Lord first attended to his physical blindness. On his sightless eyes He put clay, and sent him to wash in the pool of Siloam. The graphic record reads: "He went away therefore, and washed, and came seeing." Miraculously this man was given physical sight; but he was still spiritually blind. He was still just the same person with sight that he was without it. He did not as yet see and know Christ as Saviour. When Jesus heard that he had been cast out of the synagogue because of his unwavering testimony of all he knew about the One Who had given him sight, He found him and said: "Dost thou believe on the Son of God?" "He answered and said, And who is He, Lord, that I may believe on Him?" There He stood with the miraculous eyes looking upon the One who had given him sight, and yet he knew Him not; he had not as yet become the new man in Christ. Jesus answered his question: "Thou hast both seen Him and He it is that speaketh with thee. And he said, Lord I believe. And he worshiped Him." Immediately the new man was created. He could not have faith without its necessary perception, for without knowledge but credulity was possible. Knowing now that he was before the Son of God, a living, saving, seeing faith was possible. He believed on Him. The worshiping soul had come into being. He had been created anew. Before this he had been blind both physically and spiritually. The giving of spiritual sight had followed the giving of the physical; and the new man in Christ had arrived.

The Redeeming Creator had enabled the spiritually blind personality to see and live, to become a new person in Him and by Him.

II. The New Nature

The word "nature" is often used in the popular sense, meaning the whole physical world as distinguished from the spiritual world. Technically, nature is the inherent and distinguishing qualities and characteristics of any substance or existence. We also speak of the nature of a particular activity or force as distinguished from others.

In the realm of life and personality there are both created and directly imparted natures. Life itself has its own nature as distinguished from the non-vital. Personal nature clearly belongs to the highest realm or type of life, as already said. In the religious realm God's nature must stand first, not only in existence but also as the norm of that true both as original and final in the spiritual realm. There is therefore the godly and the ungodly, the holy and the unholy, and so on with all the moral and personal relations and characteristics within and the manifestations without. There is its own nature in everything whether personal or otherwise.

1. One of the wisest things Pres. A. H. Strong said is: "By Regeneration the governing disposition of the soul is made holy." Perhaps the largest term of character, relation and activity in the moral and spiritual is "Holy." Because fully applicable to God only, it means most in Him. It is the absolute and unapproachable in

the transcendent and perfect personal nature of God. It is the "Godness" of God, His unsmirchable character of absolute purity, the dignity of the infinitely supreme integrity of His flawless purity and endless perfection. In God *nature* has the first and foremost meaning, and gives rise to all comparative similar meanings.

Neither man nor angel nor anything else has underived holiness; for in the realm of all creation the holy is that which is normal or true to God in relation, attitude and activity. Only the personal in all creation has power to change its nature. In this self-determination of persons there may be derived or realized the unholy by and in personal becoming. Hence all holiness in man is estimated in what he is in personal likeness of character to God, whether he lives in Him or exists in living death of contrary attitude and activity toward God. Here we come upon the unescapable fact of human unholiness, godlessness, sin, or iniquity. God made man with a nature for Himself, but with power to make self an end instead of the means to the highest fulfilment in God. Failing God, man most of all fails himself. Nowhere else can ingratitude and disloyalty do him such damage. He cannot get along without God, but God is not dependent upon him. His enmity to the Most High puts his nature in ruins and breeds hopeless corruption, but for the God he forsakes.

2. Only by the Creator becoming Re-creator to man is there a ghost of hope for him. How can God cleanse unholy personal nature? With what can He cure the corruption of unholiness? By what can He renew or

regenerate the old nature into the new? This is the great inquiry to be answered by Divine Redemption.

In any case, nature is never separable from substance. The problem God has is to change the very substance of human personality. Metaphysics cries out, that cannot be done! Divine vitalism replies, it is done! Just that is the mission of Christ in Redemption, to displace death with life, and even life with more abundant living. In the last section we tried to show that it is not mere theory but history, that human persons have been changed from death unto life, brought out of the grave of sin into living correspondence with God, into conformity with His will and purposes.

By the miracle-working power of the Re-Creator and by the supernatural self-impartation of Jesus Christ the new nature and personality does come. He creates the new nature with its outstanding affinity with God. That redemption nature is pro-God and anti-iniquity. The regenerated nature is in Christ and out of the selfish self. It is the true self to self because true to God. In a word, the new nature by Redemption is Christ in us the hope of glory.

3. What says His Word about this? II Peter 1:2 ff., "Grace to you and peace be multiplied in the knowledge of God and of Jesus our Lord; seeing that His divine power hath granted unto us all things that pertain unto life and godliness, through knowledge of Him that called us by His own glory and virtue; whereby He hath granted us His precious and exceeding great promises; that through these ye may become *partakers of the*

Divine nature, having escaped the corruption that is in the world by lust." This is a supremely rich passage telling us of the partaking of the Divine nature. Let us look at the contrast pictured in Eph. 2:1 ff., "And you did He make alive when ye were dead through your trespasses and sins, wherein ye once walked according to the course of this world, according to the prince of the powers of the air, of the spirit that now worketh in the sons of disobedience; among whom we also all lived in the lusts of our flesh, doing the desires of the flesh and of the mind (thoughts) and were by nature children of wrath, even as the rest: but God made us alive together with Christ . . . and raised us up with Him, and made us to sit with Him in the heavenly places in Christ Jesus."

4. The scriptural explanation as to this change of personal nature is somewhat the same as the change which came to the Son of God by His Incarnation-begetting and birth. When our Lord talked with Nicodemus about this "birth from above," he explained (see John 3:1 ff): "That which is born of the flesh is flesh; and that which is born of the Spirit is spirit." The Greek word here means more than born. It is *gennaō,* begotten, procreated, conceived, fig. regenerated. From this it is clear that *regeneration is as truly by a supernatural conception as was that of Christ.* The same Holy Spirit by whom He was conceived begets every new-born soul or person. "Except one be born of water and the Spirit, he cannot enter into the Kingdom of God" (verse 5).

There is another important character of the New Nature, namely, *it is sinless.* But it is not exactly like Adam's nature when created, for this is re-created. It comes from the Re-Creator Who Himself had passed through the conflict with sin in His earthly life, and died at the hands of sinners. After His self-sacrifice on the cross, He gives by self-impartation or transfusion life from His Risen Person victorious over iniquity the New Nature to man which is sin-proof, sin-hating, sin-opposing, because of what it manifested itself to be in Christ's crucifixion. In this imparted New Nature from Christ there is innate repulsion to the spirit of iniquity, because the Holy Spirit not only begets this New Nature but also dwells in it.

5. The old nature, that of the flesh, is always prone to sin, ready for it, and often carries the Christian into sin. To the New Nature there is no satisfaction by iniquity. On the contrary, it is stung by it and made miserable as was Peter when he denied the Lord. All this, however, is not entirely due to the old nature, for the seductive power of Satan plays a part which betimes seems overwhelming. The old simile of the pig lolling in the mud is somewhat out of date, for we now know that instinct was guiding the hog in taking a hygienic mud-bath. But the sheep as ever avoids the mud. Falling down and bemired, it still bleats piteously for release. I John 3:9, "Whosoever is begotten of God doeth no sin, because His seed abideth in him: and he cannot sin (*with the new nature*) because he is begotten of God." 5:18, "We know that whatsoever is begotten of God sinneth not (does not keep on sin-

ning); but he that was begotten of God keepeth himself, and the evil one toucheth him not."

III. The New Life

We cannot conceive of life being manufactured. It is *transmitted.* Even in creation the Spirit of God brooded or hovered over the waters. And God breathed into man, that is imparted to him, the breath of life. Life must come from life. The new life of the new creation, or new person, must come from some life. Its character explains its source. "Marvel not that I said unto thee, Ye must be born anew" (or from above) (verse 7). Then Jesus went on to speak of the mystery of the Spirit's ministry.

1. The Holy Spirit has three great ministries: to communicate Christ, to produce holiness, and to create or sustain fulfilment-fellowship (*koinōnia*). His work it is to communicate the Christ life, impart or transfuse His spiritual blood to the believer. The fellowship of kindred life in Christ He perpetuates. He sustains this life by continuing to give of Christ. This imparted life of Christ has at least two services: to grow a soul for God, and constantly to cleanse it from all sin. The Word of the Spirit helps in this. "Now are ye clean through the word I have spoken unto you." The mind needs cleansing from evil thought. But entire personality, its whole life, needs purification, for sin attacks from every quarter. To preserve the new life intact, healthy and serviceful to God there must be adapted and competent help from Christ by the Holy Spirit.

For one thing there must be maintained and cultivated an intelligent dread and hatred of sin. We have it to fear from within, from the old nature called the "flesh." It is a wise provision that we are kept in conflict with sin at such close quarters. Why do women hate disorder and dirt more than men do? For most of them it is the every-day job to keep habitation and household free from dust and filth and to protect all else that preserves the sanitary. By the struggle in overcoming sin within our own nature and from without, God teaches us never to let die down the sense of its repulsiveness, enmity and damage to Him, ourselves, and the service to be rendered. For God cannot be well helped by dirty hands, filthy souls, defiled hearts, and minds full of contamination that corrodes as well as dulls and disables.

2. The New Life must be kept from the old sin, for there can be no new sin; only the devil's old ungodliness and selfishness. Of course it takes a lot more carefulness and vigilance and wisdom in this perpetual war with the enemy in constant contact. Here we think of that delusion from the devil, the craze of sinless perfection. Those who think themselves the chief of saints in this way are the chief of sinners; while Paul, who thought himself the chief of sinners, was really the chief of saints. When our humility is scarce, danger and decay are abundant. Sense of the seriousness of sin is one-half of the health and sanity of the Christian life. The other half, of course, is appreciation of so great a salvation, so wondrous a Saviour, so competent a God.

The fifth column enemy within is ever allied to the enemy without and ever ready to hand us over to captivity in iniquity. "We wrestle not with flesh and blood." But we must wrestle by the help of the blood of Christ that cleanses us from the defilement with which we battle. If evil spirits were a reality to Christ and battled with Him, what sort of reality is that which denies they exist? The same sort of reality they are, the reality of that evil which does most harm when thought mere delusion.

3. Was it not Luther who said, "Satan never chases a bag of chaff"; and that "we cannot prevent the birds from flying over our heads, but we can prevent them from making nests in our hair"? Some are spiritually so bald, evil would have a slippery foundation to build on their heads. Instead of a spiritual shampoo they simonize. There are heads grown so old in thinking the devil's thoughts after him, evil is no longer a temptation to them. They are what it is. They are given over to it. "He that is unrighteous, let him do unrighteousness still."

Sailors who were never off dry land, soldiers who never fought "the good fight" for a solitary second, cannot be captains in their calling. "Our wrestling . . . is against the principalities, against the powers, against the world rulers of this darkness, against the spiritual hosts of wickedness in the heavenly places." God knows what He is about in bringing us to face and to fight His foes and ours. The God for Whom we never fight is a futility to us. And then our lives would be futile, and we false. The better our lives, the severer the conflict. So was it with Christ, only He had no battle with evil within. If we were within as He was, we would have been crucified or killed long ago. Evidently as Christ could not be spared the conflict with evil, neither can we escape it and be true children of God and become the order of personality so precious to Him, so prized by Him, and for which in Christ He has paid so great a price.

4. Life in such a world as this must fight its foes or perish. But there is something more to do than battle with enemies. We must "grow up in all things into Him," and "grow in the grace and knowledge of our Lord and Saviour Jesus Christ." Every life has its environment in which it is rooted, from which it derives its nourishment, and which enables it to do its work, bear its fruit, fulfil its mission. The Christian has his Divine environment and his human. Being personal this life must be adjusted to other persons according to their normal relation to us. Whom Christ cannot keep company with, we cannot do more. There are many sorts of fellowship, good and bad. We cannot have our Saviour as Lord unless He is Lord over and in our fellowships. He is the newest because He is always first. He never takes second place, where He does not belong; and where He does not belong, He does not fit. And neither do we! We should not only seek first the kingdom of God, but seek first the King of that kingdom; otherwise we shall not find it.

In the personal life love is the most important outgo. That tells what we do with ourselves, and where we go. He Who loved us and came unto us to solve the problem of our Redemption, calls us to come unto Him, labor for Him, and find rest in Him. There is a sense in which love of the Lord is a perpetual coming unto Him in response to His love and His perpetual coming unto us. Love is the most living thing with which we have to do. The more love we give to the Lord who is our life, the more life we shall have and live.

5. Another important thing to which attention here may be called, is the double ministry of the blood of Christ. This is the transfusion which gives and sustains spiritual or Christian life, and the other ministry is that of the constant cleansing from sin. The first is the constant supply of the vital impartation of Christ Himself to the new nature that it may not only live but bear fruit, even as the sap of the vine feeds the branch. To the old unredeemed nature of the "flesh" there can be none of this vital transfusion because unregenerate. The re-created nature of human personality needs the ministry of the spiritual blood of Christ to animate it, that the regenerated person may live unto Him, maintain its integrity, and do its work.

First then there is the service of the blood of Christ to save the sinner; and next that which makes and keeps the saint a saint. Near the beginning of the century I recall that on the second page of the British Weekly Dr. David Smith regularly contributed a column. His words on living by the blood of Christ have long since left me; but I recall his thought more or less accurately. There is, he said, only one way to live truly the Christian life, viz. by coming every morning of every day to the cross of Christ, to the crucified and risen Saviour. Not a day have we lived that we "have already attained or are made perfect." Not a day has passed without its sins of omission and of commission needing the cleansing of the blood of Christ. John says that if we say we live altogether without sin, we lie and the truth is not in us. Then we but add to our sin, instead of confessing it, and being cleansed from it.

Chapter Eleven

UNION WITH CHRIST

Introduction

Union with Christ is the largest and most accurate definition of vital Christian relation. This is the highest, deepest and broadest unity we shall ever know by experience. It is a unity closely related to that of the triune Godhead, for it is the pattern and spirit of the union of the Trinity carried into the whole outreach of redemption. Union with Christ is the heart and soul of vital contact in the new relation of life in Him.

On the human side the foundation of union with Christ is laid in regeneration. (1) The regenerated person is the begotten of the Lord by the Holy Spirit. The Lord may enter into union with His own, and through Him they who are His are united with the entire Trinity. (2) This new life springs from the redeeming life of Christ.

Union with Christ lays also the foundation for sacrificial personality and the life therewith. Cause must equal effect and be of a kind with it. The sacrificial union of Christ with those born again goes on to realize Christian personality and its sacrificial life and service.

Union with the great Sacrificial Self in Christ is the constant cure for self-for-self realization. It guarantees that all resultant undertakings will not only be worth while but also worthily performed. With the never-failing Christ as the sacrificial Source through which we are in vital union, we are assured that the Risen Life will lift us above all failures and discouragements. As Rom. 6:5 puts it: "For if we have become united with Him in the likeness of His death, we shall be also in the likeness of His resurrection."

I. The Genius of Union with Christ

1. It is first of all a personal union. All that personality means in the Redeemer-Person of the Son of God, and all it means in the redeemed and regenerated follower goes into that union. In the Trinity we learn that the three Divine Persons are distinct but complementary. They are other-conscious inter-personalities. They are inseparably and infinitely social as well as eternally sacrificial in relation to each other. Their immeasurable peace and harmony is the sure answer as to what becomes of the warmongers of this world so utterly out of agreement with or adjustment to them. God having invested not only His likeness and image but also the Christ Himself in human souls, there is thereby constituted a place for humanity within the very harmony and unity of the Godhead-life.

2. Its Genius is also manifest in the vital character of union with Christ. Life has its deepest, vastest, purest and best meaning in the Holy Trinity. That is, of course, uncreated, unlimited (except by each other),

and perfect life carried up to that infinity corresponding to their personal existence. There is, as Paul tells us, "a savor of life unto life" as well as "a savor of death unto death." Any personality dead to life in God cannot find an atom of spiritual life anywhere else. Then it is death unto death to pass by the redemption by life Divine which alone can restore lifeless human life. The character of this union in Christ goes down as deep as the unfailing character of His sacrificial love, and mounts up as high as the highest heavens. There can be no imitation of it. The integrity of that union is in genius like the Holiness of God—without a parallel.

3. The genius of the mind or mental phase of this union is the truth as it is in Jesus absorbed and organized into redeemed personality. And there is no truth anywhere for us which is not an offspring of the mind of the Son of God, Who is the truth of God on every side. There is a whole world of thought, idea, and truth itself springing out of the meaning and vitality of this oneness in Christ. There is an order of mind for man without rival that is the intellectual power of that union-life. The sacred Scriptures sprang out of that union in inspiration. The thought and mind and utterance in union with Christ has its Divine side and its human side. We have the greater richness of it in the Word; but we have the richest and best of it on the human side as compared with all other human mind and thought and expression.

4. There is the constitutional character of union in Christ. There is that which constitutes it, and that which it constitutes. We speak of a man with a good constitution; but no man has the best constitution who is a stranger to that union in Redemption. The sacrificial love of God by Incarnation and Redemption reached out to lost humanity with the very foundation of all that is good gone from it, and put the foundation of the Rock of Ages under it, and the constitution of the Incarnate Son of God into it, and made its Redemption inherent with the love of Christ which passeth knowledge.

That which constitutes this union is the coming together of God in Redemption finding man sick and weary with his sins. It is union at the greatest price ever built by the Blood of Sacrifice. Well does the Bible term "eternal Redemption" that accomplished by it. Its very constitution is laid deep in the nature of God. When this universe shall be reduced to foam on the shores of eternity, that union with Christ shall have risen far above "the wrecks of time" and enable us to dwell in infinite security in the habitation of God.

5. Christ's self-giving is the genius of union in, and reciprocation with Christ; it is the sacred secret of this mutuality. But Christ gave all the riches of His glorious, Divine, sacrificial Personality, while all we had to give in return was the poverty of the beggary of the misery of lost and ruined and lifeless, sinful wretchedness.

On the other hand it was the extreme bitterness and

degradation of our lost estate which gave meaning to the riches of salvation, the provision of the closest personal union with the King of Glory, the Son of God. It was that reciprocating or responding naked poverty and starvation which took from the outstretched hand of Christ, the bread and water of life, the milk of His Word, and the clothing for our nakedness.

There is the personal reciprocation of appreciation when the sinner is saved, the diseased healed, the blind made to see, the ignorant made to know, the unhappy brought into endless joy. But the best of all appreciation is that lived out, just as the best thanksgiving is thanksliving. No marriage union amounts to much without constant reciprocity of appreciation be it for the daily ever-so-little favors. So is it in the Christian life made glad in giving joy to the Lord by constant appreciation; for He is ever doing things so essential, though minute, that we miss the most of them entirely, and so large that we lack sense of proportion to evaluate them fully.

6. Appropriation, the genius of union with Christ, is to the repenting sinner most visible. All created life has its power of appropriation. And there is a sense in which the divine has also this power of appropriation, but it appropriates only what belongs to it or is given to it. After all, this is true of the truly Christian life also. We are redeemed unto redemption, saved unto receiving all the blessings and favors of salvation.

Here is where union with Christ is far from being overworked, even if this were possible. He has infinitely more for us than we know how to receive. Now this union is meant to be access unto and into the things Christ has for those who love Him. If our powers of appropriation by mind and heart and faith and love were equal to the riches and gifts God in Christ has for us, we would be no more weak, sickly and undeveloped Christian persons.

To appropriate in the Christian life is far more than to receive. It is receiving with divine wisdom. It is taking the bread of greatness that we can digest, laying hold on what we can well use for God and the good of those around us. Appropriation true to union with Christ means appropriating that appropriate to our needs, our tasks, our situation in service. There are promises in the Word of God never meant for us. People in entirely different situations need them. Too often we go to church for strong meat and get pap meant for spiritual little ones. Oh, to know how to appropriate the great things of God for the Christian life, and so to become greater souls, greater sympathizers, greater builders, and bigger boosters for the Kingdom of God.

7. The genius of union with Christ also lies in its substance. Now, union is both state and activity. The substance of response to a state is conformity to it, and its activity is the action called for by the genius of this union. We cannot be in union with Christ while He is going in one direction and we in the opposite. We are not in union with Him by the things that tend to disrupt our service to Christ and to His own needy ones. Perhaps we are often non-conformists with that to which we should conform, and conformists with that

directly contrary to the genius of union with the Lord. Are we stubborn with the Lord and pliable in the hands of sin? Iniquity may not completely dissolve that union, but it certainly is no help to it. When the very substance of our lives is taken to be this unity with the Redeemer, then we conform to His will, to His cleansing power, and keep disintegrators out by the Holy Spirit, the Spirit of manifest consecration to the Master.

II. The Characteristic Activity of Union with Christ

1. Faith is one of the earliest activities of this union. For that matter, faith is a primary or pioneer power whether in good or in evil. There is a sinful faith which leads to the opposite of this union. That sort is either ungodly or selfish faith. Faith in the Lord Jesus Christ is unifying. It brings Him to the soul, as well as brings the soul to Him. Until the unsaved one has somewhat of the faith in Christ that Christ has in Himself as Redeemer, there can be no real union. To the new life there must be the new faith. The new nature is in part the nature of faith in Christ as Saviour. There can be no real unity while personal faiths are in conflict. A man might offer us a thousand compliments. If he couples them with, "But I don't believe in you," his praises would form no basis of unity. Faith is that in all life which is the rooting in and the laying hold upon the soil, or the corresponding activity in reciprocity between the life and its environment. Faith unites whether the life be low or high, whether im-

personal or personal. Even a dog can tell whether you have faith in him or not. Personal faith in a Redeemer is faith in the Saviour for what He professes to be and what He offers to do.

2. Interest is also an activity close to faith and to desire. It has unity in proportion as the interest is identical with faith. Christ is mightily interested in the lost soul. He seeks to make known His interest and also the Redemption He offers. When this lost one becomes interested in Christ and what He offers in Salvation, then the union between them begins. Every life, good or bad, has its interests in correspondence with its nature or character. After all, one could measure the extent of union between a human person and Christ by the extent and character of interests they have in common. Union with Christ must tend to bring us to share in His great interests. In one way interests are the currents of life. When two streams of interest converge and unite, the union is in the flood resulting. Of course, Christ has much greater and much better interests than we have. The enlargement of our lives and our persons results from union with Him in His vast interests. They tend to lift us up and out in their realms and achievements.

3. Other activities of one's union with Christ are those characteristic of both persons in it. The adroit strategy of the evil one is to lead us into works which do not correspond with the nature of this union. This could only tend to weaken the reciprocal indwelling which is the soul of union with Christ. All activity

growing out of being possessed by our Lord and out of His possession of us contribute to the intensity and growth of union with Him. There is no union without its reciprocal indwelling, and no indwelling without its possession. The activity of all reciprocal impartation comes from the union in indwelling. The law of the triune activity of the Godhead is in some measure paralleled in the law of activity between Christ and the soul with which He is in union.

III. Reciprocal Desires in Process of Union

The responsive process of reciprocal desires is an important feature of union with Christ. These are the hungers of the human soul on the one side and the yearnings of the Saviour on the other, for the same things.

1. The human desire to know more of Christ is symptomatic of genuineness and health. No soul can be in real union with Christ and not desire to know Him better. We cannot be as the little child who after attending school the first day said, "Mother, I don't need to go to school any more. I learned everything the teacher told me." The best school of Christ is union with Him. He has much to teach us, and each day there are the things to remember and the things to acquire. There are many things to learn from the textbook of experience; and many from the Word; and also many things direct from the Master Himself. What we receive from each of these helps us to acquire from the other two. The true way to be still and know that Christ is Lord, is to let Him have a chance to

tell us the many things He has to say unto us. Life would be far different, our union with Christ not so silent, if we desired intently to hear Him directly. We may so seldom practice the presence of the Lord, we are apt to think it a strange doctrine that He can and does speak to us. Union with Christ is not to render Him dumb to us, but to enable Him to speak to us whenever He will, and to hear us in glad and often to us unexpected response.

2. There is on the human side of this union the desire to enter more fully into it, more fully to lay hold of Christ and His promises, to comply more completely with His wishes, to coöperate more deeply and extensively with His will. One thing sure to come with real desire to coöperate completely with Christ is to discover how vastly beyond us He is in every way that is good, and how meagre are as yet the best of our attainments in Him. Sanity, common sense and spiritual uncommon sense when we possess them, makes us feel our unworthiness and littleness of attainment as compared with what He is. What utter madness to think we "have attained or are already made perfect," when the nearer we get to Christ the further off we seem to be from what He is in all respects of perfect Personality with the Father and with the Holy Spirit. A perfectionist intoxicated with the verbosity of his superabundance of self-esteem said: "For seventeen years I have not once sinned. Each Saturday night I cast up accounts with Christ; and sometimes I find myself in debt to Him, and other times that He is in

debt to me." Which does the blessed Lord do, laugh or weep on hearing this?

3. On the human side there is further the desire to love Christ fully, such as He deserves to be loved and has loved us, to give ourselves to Him with utter unrestraint, to possess Him yet more and to be far more possessed by Him than in the past. Perhaps one reason why we do not make more advance in Christ is that either we are too easily satisfied with ourselves, or we have a meagre appetite for attainment in union with Him. It is all right to have the peace that passeth understanding as to our being saved and accepted of the Lord; but our peace with our imperfections, our failures, our stupidity and slowness of apprehending the things of Christ should pass far beyond our understanding that we do have such. Alas, the river of our love for Him often descends to a mere trickle between the dry rocks of our selfish interests. Would to God that our degrees in societies and universities were infinitely surpassed with degrees of fellowship with Christ and attainments in the super-school of the Master of men and all creation. Some earthly fellowships are dead weights to fellowship with Christ; and some of the diplomas of advancement in human learning may but measure the extent of unbelief in the supernatural and its Christ. Better the tiniest advance in union with Him than all the pitiable progress in really getting further from Him in inability to measure His stature and fulness.

4. On the side of Christ in this union there is His desire to have, to own, to possess those for whom He

has died, to impart Himself to them, and to perfect them. These are more important desires than ours, or even than our desires to see the lost come to Him. *Christ's desires are like Him,* and He is in every good way bigger and better than we are. He is perfection in union with imperfection. He is wholly sacrificial, while we are not yet utterly rid of selfishness. He is steady and faithful, holy and pure. He has paid in Himself the price of our Redemption. In this union with us He seeks its impartation to us. He is the executor of His will on our behalf, and He is seeking to have its utmost provisions and riches and Redeeming merits become ours. His desires do not necessarily conflict with ours, except as ours are sinful. Of course, a great feature of His Redemption is to sanctify all natural desire, to originate and perfect all Godward or spiritual ones. When Paul says, "My heart's desire and prayer to God for Israel is, that they might be saved," he was doubly inspired. The desire was inspired of God, and the writing of it was also inspired. No one is ever inspired of God to deny the inspiration of God. Jesus told Peter, "Satan hath desired to have you, that he might sift you as wheat." Then the Lord went on to say, "But I have prayed for thee that thy faith fail not." It was Peter's union with Christ that saved him from an utter collapse. How many times has Christ asked the Father for us and thus saved us—all except the chaff! Self-sufficiency and its desires are certainly not wheat. Far better the Lord's desires and prayers for us than our own desires and even our own prayers.

IV. Diagnosis of the Condition of Union

We have been diagnosing desire, whether it be of God, or of the devil, or of ourselves as affecting our union with Christ. There is also possible a general diagnosis of the condition of this union with Christ.

1. We may inquire at any time how *strong*, how *steady*, and how *secure* it is. On the side of Christ it is always the three at once and many others. We feel the pulse of a sick one, and thereby to some extent by the strength or character of the arterial throb, judge of the person's physical condition. How blessedly the Master kept His finger on the pulse of the disciples' spiritual condition. He knew what was in man, and what his condition was in every way. He is the Great Judge of all men. He feels as well as knows the spiritual condition of every one of us. Many a doctor feels all he knows; and some save themselves by knowing much more than they feel. Christ has exhaustless resources in Himself to feel for us in sympathy equally with what He knows about the state of our union with Him. For all belonging to Him He is the stability, the strength, and the security of that vital union with them. As it was with Peter, it does not all depend upon us. The Almighty Saviour supplements our many weaknesses. He is the Great Physician to remedy our infirmities.

2. *The kind of life we live,* how willing or how wilful we are in relation to our Lord, how fully are we committed to His plans and purposes for us, and how robust or weak or sickly are we, are pertinent

questions that may be asked concerning them and all that affecting the state of our union with Him. There is also the question as to the growth of Christ's power of attraction over us, and our affinity with Him. The lion has affinity for the lamb. This, however, is not in the lamb's interest. There are the powers that would destroy or consume us. Sometimes we are like the lamb offering to brush the lion's teeth. Often we do tempt the devil. Were it not for the oversight of the Lord, the blessed pull of union with Him which draws us away from danger or destruction, we could not survive. It is a good thing that in this as in all else for our good, there is no limit to the self-giving of the Saviour to whom we are vitally united. There is limit, however, to our power of absorption, of appropriating out of His fulness, from which to receive is to live and grow and survive. There should be increase of self-committal to Christ, for He is our inseparable hope and recourse. I Cor. 6:17, "But he that is joined unto the Lord is one spirit." In the nineteenth verse, "Know ye not that your body is a temple of the Holy Spirit which is in you, which ye have from God? and ye are not your own; for ye were bought with a price: glorify God therefore in your body."

On Christ's side this union with Him never fails. On our side the question may often arise, "Are we really in Christ? Perhaps there is no expression of union with the Lord in the New Testament occurring more often than or as often as this—"In Christ." Strange as it may sound, Christ is bound to be more certainly and deeply in us than we are in Him. There is more room in Him for us, than in us for Him.

V. The History of Union with Christ

Each person has his own history. If a follower of Christ, there is the history of his Christian life; and most significant in this is the history of what has happened in and to his union with the Lord. Each tree has its history, and bears the marks of the storms and other things which have affected it. Our Master used the vine as an apt illustration of vital spiritual union with Him (John XV): "I am the true vine and my Father is the husbandman. . . . Abide in me, and I in you. As the branch cannot bear fruit of itself, except it abide in the vine, so neither can ye, except ye abide in me. I am the vine, ye are the branches: He that abideth in me, and I in him, the same beareth much fruit: for apart from me ye can do nothing."

1. The history of the branch in relation to the vine has special value as Christ's own illustration. It is vital. It is the story of its life. So with the Christian. His relation to his Saviour is vital, for it is the account of the state of his union with the Lord which gives life. There are contactual and structural problems. The branch in the vine not in the contactual way is not structurally or vitally adjusted or united with the main stem to draw its sap and bear its fruit. On the other hand, the vine is useless without its branches. Christ has no other way of bearing the fruit of evangelism except by those who know Him. If they fail Him, He has no other provision. So the union with

Christ which gives the possibility of winning the lost is a most strategic thing both ways, for both the branches and the vine. That point of contact between Christ and the Christian is supremely important. The history of how it has functioned, tells the story of receding or advancing in the evangelistic enterprise which is the most important on earth. Of course, there are other things to be done in the Christian life besides the winning of men to Christ. Christian education is important, if it is Christian! If it becomes dominated by anti-Christian science, philosophy, and unspiritual social service, it is then a most serious drawback to Christian progress.

2. Touching all of these points is our history as to attitude and use of the Word of God, whether the intelligence that educates this union on the human side is from heaven or from earth. I have called attention elsewhere[26] that the fruitfulness of preaching depends upon faithfulness to the Word that allows no substitution of the wisdom of man. God has promised that "His Word will not return unto Him void." There is no such promise for any other word. How could there be, for any other word instead of returning to God gets further and further away from Him by the gravitation of inadequacy and perversion? So it comes to pass that in all the Christian centuries the esteem and use of God's own Word in the Scriptures marks the measure of the Church's usefulness and power to win the lost, and also to maintain the fidelity of being true witnesses for God in such a world as this. It is

[26] "Inspiration Explains Itself," Foreword.

never true intelligence nor the Mind of the Spirit that fails to use the message of the Scriptures. Back through the years the intensifying or the slackening in service, the intelligence of God or the foolishness of this world's wisdom, tell most clearly and significantly the direction of the movement of Christian life and activity. It does show that what is esteemed among men as the foolishness of God is wiser than the wisdom of men. The weakness of the poorest Christian has the greatest strength in existence guarding, seeking and ministering to him.

VI. Effects and Effectiveness

We have been considering the effects and the effectiveness of the strategic matter of faithfulness to union with Christ. That has just been dealt with in a general way concerning the state of the Church. Here we wish to conclude with the individual and personal condition in this matter.

1. Nothing more pertains to *efficiency* in the personal Christian life than nearness to Christ; and nothing can so well secure, establish and use that nearness as this union with Christ, which is assuredly the ministry of His self-giving constantly. To the soul really and truly born of God there is bound to be a healthful yearning for what is expressed in the fine old hymn, "Nearer my God to Thee." True, we are spiritually well situated in union with Christ, if we are His; but this union is so sweet and satisfying, and so menaced by the world and the enemy of souls, we are ever yearning for the nearer nearness in the closer and yet closer

union with Him. He tugs at our heartstrings. The world tugs at our unsanctified desires, appetites and interests. Hence there is a good deal of straying and wandering. If we are His, we are never wholly out of touch with Christ, not to our credit but to His, for He never leaves us nor forsakes us. How could He depart from us with ever so small area of union with us? By faithful union with Christ, keeping in touch with Him, is the secret of real efficiency in His service.

2. Wisdom, Control and Fellowship are personal effects of this union in Christ and with Him. There are the three ministries to our sorely needed wisdom—the Word, the Holy Spirit, and union with Christ, and the greatest of these is the last. All of these three bring us the wisdom that cometh from above. Even the best of knowledge is not wisdom, for wisdom lies in wisely using our knowledge.

Christ's control of us is all one with fellowship with us. Fellowship with Him is always subservience to the will of Christ. His will and ours come together, when they do come, by union with our blessed Lord. And here is why we ever need the wisdom of preferring His way to our own, and His fellowship to any other on earth. His fellowship is heaven let down to earth, our souls to greet, and make glad and greater and sweeter.

3. Growth, Grasp and Fulfilment of Sonship are three more of the many effects which come by vital, contactual and structural union with our life-source Saviour. The best and most enduring growth is that of Life Eternal; and this is always ministered or im-

parted to us by the One in Redemptive union with us unto Life Eternal. Seldom do we stop to realize that Eternal Life to be that must be Eternal Growth. Then, will we know ourselves after a billion years in glory? Thank God that we have all eternity to grow in, and this in the holiest, highest, richest life,—for we cannot find enough adjectives with our finite minds to portray this chief of imparted infinities.

Every part of our personal nature has its own grasp. There is apprehension of the mind, grasp of heart, grip of faith, embrace of soul, and laying hold on fellowships. Probably there is no such grasp as that by our union with Christ. It grips us in the deepest and by the strongest. And, blessed be God, it grips Christ too. By and through and in Him we are grasped with an eternal hold of fellowship with the entire Trinity. Our union with Christ is really our union with the whole Godhead.

In this deepest way of all we have our fellowship with the Father. And this fellowship comes from our fulfilment in the Father's purposes concerning us. The Son along with the Holy Spirit are the great effective Agents of Divine Fulfilment. By union with Christ we are Sons of God, and in that Sonship we have fellowship with the Father, indwelling of the Holy Spirit, and oneness with and by Him who redeemed us.

Chapter Twelve

THE INHABITATION BY THE HOLY SPIRIT

Introduction

There is the old Trinitarian explanation that God the Father is God over us; God the Son is God for us; and God the Holy Spirit is God in us. It would be better to say that the Father is specially God over us, and the Son is specially God for us, and the Holy Spirit is specially God in us. The Son and the Holy Spirit also are ever over us. The Father and the Holy Spirit are ever for us. And the Father and the Son ever dwell in us.

The Holy Trinity is such that wherever one of its Persons is, the other two cannot be absent; and whatever one of the Divine Persons does, the other two share in coöperation with Him. Hence they all cooperate in helping each other in their respective offices. It is an untrue explanation of Redemption that the Son suffered on the Cross while the Father and the Holy Spirit were mere spectators or, worse, even penalizers. That interpretation would utterly destroy the character, nature, relations and genuineness of the Holy Trinity. While the Son was on the Cross, the Father was there with Him with the Cross in His heart, and the Holy Spirit was there in the Son as ever in unlimited measure. This view does not abolish the Godhead to save some theory of so-called "atonement."

1. Which is more precious to us, the three inseparable Persons of the Trinity, or some theory of the Cross that shatters completely the integrity of the infinite Personal unity of the Godhead? Any theory which does that is not stating a divine necessity, but instead the conjured up requirement of the theory itself. *The first necessity of the Godhead is that it remain intact.* Without this no Redemption is possible. There can be no sacrifice of the Son that sacrifices the eternal unity of the three Persons composing the Trinity. In the chapter to follow some of the scriptures taken to mean a separation, not to say, desertion, of the One in that agony of the death of all deaths, will be examined at some length. Here we study the ministry of the Holy Spirit in relation to the Father and the Son.

I. The Spirit's Ministry in Relation to the Godhead

1. Personality in the Godhead is in many ways higher and greater than human personality. The Persons of the Trinity are infinite and inter-existent, while we are finite and co-existent. We are separable from one another. We can be in the same place as each other, or we can be in some other place. If divine personality were not inter-existent, one infinite Personality would take up all the room. They are also uncreated and eternal. We are created and had a beginning. Once

we were not. There never was a time when the Father, the Son and the Holy Spirit were not. The unity of these Divine Persons is also quite as eternal. The tri-unity is structural and yet it is infinitely personal. Our unity is not primarily structural. It may exist, or it may not. But our unity is always co-personal, not constitutionally inter-personal, like that of the Trinity.

2. The unity of the Godhead is as much higher and greater than that of humanity as the Godhead is higher and greater than humanity. We have, not a constitutional and inter-personal unity, but a co-personal and coöperative unity. The Persons of the Trinity are infallibly and eternally coöperative on a higher level and in a much larger way than we can coöperate with each other. To some extent we are complementary persons, that is, to some degree we complete each other's personalities. We are a race of male and female persons. In the Trinity no sex is possible for it is not a race. There are persons in it but no individuals. That is, there are no separable persons in it. The individual is as far as we can go to divide up the race. Individual means in, *not;* dividual, *dividable.* The Godhead can never be divided in the individual ways of separate or completely separable persons. There are still other ways in which Divine Personality and the human differ. The Divine is eternally and completely realized in personality. We are always in process of personal growth by self-determination, or self-realization or personal becoming. Not long ago a book from one of our great universities said: "Two things we know about divine personality: it is self-consciousness and

self-determination." Properly, self-consciousness constitutionally belongs to selfish personality. Divine personality is other-conscious because the three eternally belong to each other in perfect accord of love and self-sacrifice. Their unity is an eternal harmony of three lives in the perfectly complementary unity of one indivisible entity. God is one Being of three complementary Other-Selves. As to self-determination God is the eternally determined in personality because uncreated, infinite and eternal."

While the three Persons of the Trinity are absolutely the same in substance, they are not equal in office, from the very nature of office. For example, the Son is the Word, the Expression, the Revelation of the Father. Now, the Revelation or Expression must be forever subject to that revealed or expressed. In office, therefore, the Son is forever subordinate to the Father, even as the Spirit is to the Son.

3. There was the time when the Roman Catholic and the Greek Catholic Churches came to differ about the Holy Spirit, the former holding that He proceeded from both the Father and the Son, and the latter claiming that He proceeded from the Father only. Perhaps there is a sense in which both were right. The Holy Spirit may proceed forth from the Father in some things in a way that He does not from the Son, as for example, in the Incarnation. But there is no question that the Son can, and does, send the Holy Spirit; and He sends Him in redemptive self-communication as well. We may therefore say that in office or work the Holy Spirit is subject to both the Father and the

Son; and that the Son even in His great Self-sacrifice of Redemption was subject to the Father. In this also we see the impossibility of the Son being separated from the Father and the Holy Spirit in a self-sacrifice directed as well as appointed by the Father. And His self-sacrifice is such that the Holy Spirit must always be its Spirit and at its heart, inhabiting it and dwelling in Him.

4. In John 16:13 Jesus explains that the Holy Spirit is subject to Him in what He says. The Authorized Version wrongly translated this passage, making *apo* (*aph heautou*) mean "of Himself." The preposition here really means "from," as the Revised Version has it. "Of" might do if given the right sense, namely, on His own authority, or on His own responsibility. Thayer[27] says about this phrase, "*aph heautou*," "an expression especially common in John, of himself, from His own disposition or judgment, as distinguished from another's instruction." Then the passage should read: "Howbeit when He, the Spirit of Truth, is come, He shall guide you into all the truth: for He shall *not* speak from Himself (on His own authority); but what things soever He shall hear, these shall He speak. . . . He shall glorify me: for He shall take of mine, and shall declare it unto you. All things whatsoever the Father hath are mine: therefore said I, He taketh of mine and shall declare it unto you."

5. The foregoing passage beautifully shows the triune relation of the Godhead, and also the relation of subjection of the Holy Spirit to the Son and to the

[27] Greek-English Lexicon, p. 59.

Father. As I have said elsewhere, the Holy Spirit is God the Inhabitant. In the service and at the direction of the Father and the Son He inhabits wheresoever they send Him so to do. As Ephesians 2:22 puts it, "In whom (the Lord) ye also are builded together for a habitation of God in the Spirit."

Here the Church is specially in mind. As the Father reveals Himself through the Son, so the Son by the Holy Spirit reveals Himself through the Church. So the Holy Spirit has three habitations—in the Father, in the Son, and in the Church of the followers of Christ. The Church and the individual Christians are as incomplete without the Holy Spirit as a home would be empty with not a soul living in it. A church without the Holy Spirit is a body without its own soul.

II. The Holy Spirit's Ministry in Relation to the Church

At Pentecost the call was to repent and be baptized in Christ's name unto (*eis,* to the end of) the remission of sins and to receive the gift of the Holy Spirit. In Eph. 5:18 there is the direct command, "Be filled with (in) the Holy Spirit." John 14:17, "Even the Spirit of truth . . . for He abideth with you, and shall be in you."

1. As believers we come to Christ for Redemption and Justification to make us sons of God: then He sends the Holy Spirit for our Regeneration and Sanctification to become the servants of God. The Holy Spirit does not always come with exactly the same purpose. First He comes to *constitute* the Christian by

the impartation of the New Life and nature. Next He comes as a *Gift*, the Gift of Himself, and to bring to the Christian His personal gifts. This results in the gifts of the Spirit — love, joy, peace, faith, etc.

It seems rather inconsistent that we should perpetuate water-baptism and abandon the baptism of the Holy Spirit. Some think of the apostolic period as transitory in character and significance, having only ideal presence, powers and experience of the Spirit of God which were to pass away with the apostles and their time. This is not the teaching of the Scriptures. Christ promised that His ascent to the Father should be followed by the coming of the Second Paraclete, the Holy Spirit, who would enter upon His enduring ministry with all its blessings and gifts.

2. It is well to note further that our Lord entered upon His ministry after the Holy Spirit descended upon Him. In Isa. 11:2, it was prophesied that, "The Spirit of Jehovah shall rest upon Him, the spirit of wisdom and understanding, the spirit of counsel and might, the spirit of knowledge and of the fear of Jehovah." We may note also that then as now the Holy Spirit was the *Divine Impartation Executive.* John, the water-baptizer, explained concerning Jesus, the Spirit-baptizer: "Upon whomsoever thou shalt see the Spirit descending and abiding upon Him, the same is He that baptizeth in the Holy Spirit." This closely corresponds with Matt. 3:11, "I indeed baptize you in water unto repentance: but He that cometh after me is mightier than I, whose shoes I am not worthy to

bear: He shall baptize you in the Holy Spirit and in fire."

3. Even in Christ's experience as soon as He received the baptism of the Spirit, it brought on conflict with the evil one. Mark uses the extreme expression that He was "driven of the Spirit" into the wilderness, but the other accounts say He was "led up of the Spirit" to be tempted of the devil. So it seems that baptism of the Holy Spirit is not a protection from, but equipment for, the battle with the powers of evil. And the strategic thing in that conflict is maintaining what the Book of the Spirit teaches. For any soldier of Christ the battle is gained or lost at that point. If Satan can get him to put the question mark after the Word of God, the victory is with the tempter. In the past fifty years Satan has made more inroads there into the Christian faith than at any other point.

Having utterly defeated the devil, Christ enters upon His ministry with the announcement that, "The Spirit of the Lord is upon me, for He annointed me to preach good tidings to the poor; He hath sent me to bind up the broken-hearted, to proclaim release to the captives, and recovering of sight to the blind; to set at liberty them that are bruised, to proclaim the acceptable year of the Lord" (Luke 4: 18, 19). The Holy Spirit who thus wrought in Christ, works in the selfsame way in His followers. The same Holy Spirit who inhabited His Person, we need to dwell in us, if we are to work as faithfully as He did, and accomplish what He has given us to do.

4. We must not pass over the fact that the baptism

of the Spirit is *in fire*. This, we take it, is to set our souls on fire for God and keep them blazing with steady, dependable flame. The only persons fit for such a world of darkness as this, are those inhabited of the Holy Spirit, having His light within, and glowing with the flame of divine devotion.

5. There are these two divinely complementary things, the inhabitation of the Spirit and union with Christ; for the indwelling of the Holy Spirit enables union with Christ to be manifest in bearing fruit unto life eternal. After having supernaturally united us to Himself, the greatest thing Christ can do for us is to give us His Holy Spirit to dwell in us as divinely fruitful members of His body, the Church of His commission — and ours. Without this complementary counterpart of Christ and the Spirit, the Church is utterly unequipped, no matter what else it may possess. That is the divine adjustment to our difficult situation in the world. On the one hand, the easiest people to get along with are those most controlled by God and the Spirit. On the other hand, there are those who have the complete victory without personal quarrels but maintaining the great and good fight of faith. These are armed with union with Christ and inhabited by the Spirit of God.

In the Church this fire of the Spirit melts and consumes certain evil and destructive elements; and is therefore a refining agent purifying and separating by penetration. The same fire which destroys evil welds together the good. This Holy Fire maintains the right spiritual temperature, contacts the Spirit's motor power, and protects the Church as with a wall of fire from the contamination and infection of the world.

The Church on earth never sees the Kingdom of God as it appears to Christ unless the Holy Spirit fully dwells in the members thereof. The natural man is utterly unable to see the Kingdom of God, and therefore unable to serve it. Only the Church of Spirit-conceived or Spirit-begotten members can help Christ build and maintain His Kingdom. Calling out the non-born-again membership for this work is like sending blind men to battle.

The Spirit-filled membership of the Church is the effective body with adequate spiritual resources. Out of them flow the rivers of living waters, for the full life flows through the souls full of the Holy Spirit.

6. For effectiveness in the work of the Church nothing quite compares with *the practical power* of the Holy Spirit. He is God always at work. He is the unresting, eternally untiring, forever-going-forth Person of the Holy Trinity. As often said, He cannot dwell in either member or Church itself as water in a pitcher, but as water being poured forth as through a conduit pipe. He abides with us by going forth from us. The Church must be a river of the Water of Life, or it is not a vital body at all, but instead a stagnant pool of infection. When empty the vessel had better not go forth that way, tempting the enemy to smash it; rather it should abide for the "filling." Moses waited some forty years before he could set out on the great work God had for him. The very promises of God are empty to those who do not wait for their fulfilment.

Says Isa. 64:4, "A God . . . who worketh for him that waiteth for Him." The same God of Divine wisdom keeps one waiting forty years, while another almost instantly receives the infilling of the power from on high. The timetable of God's program is visible only on the heavenward side. This is where the Spirit has little to do with those who spend their time trying to turn heaven upside down to get at God's exact program for the future. The Holy Spirit has not come so much to reveal heaven's timetable, as to fit and keep us busy preparing persons for heaven. The hidden date of the Parousia means that the Holy Spirit has a visible date with us now and until then to fill out what remains to be done, that idle hands may not offer the Coming One their empty greetings. The hands "filling up that which is lacking of the afflictions of Christ," will not be empty for the Parousia. The best preparation for the Second Coming is to let the Holy Spirit possess us fully by His First Coming and His Constant Filling.

A necessary if not the adequate power for evangelism is without question that of the Holy Spirit. The Church, its ministry and members receive this power, but it never ceases to be the *dunamis* (power) of the Holy Ghost. Ye shall receive this power after that the Holy Spirit is come upon you. What a transformation in this and other ways resulted from the descent of the Promised Holy Spirit on that "Birthday of the Church."

7. Real evangelism can be carried on only by miraculous means, the supernatural power of the Holy Spirit in possession of the persons who thus are equipped to do this supernatural service. This is the

"great grace" that came upon the disciples who had tarried obediently at Jerusalem for the promised fulfilment of the new relation of Christ to them through His Executive, the Spirit of God. It was not hard to win with the omnipotent Holy Spirit. There is no power of man or demon which can resist that outrush and onslaught of the might of heaven, when the Sword of the Spirit, the Word of God, is wielded by the Holy Spirit to slay unbelief. The Word of God may be both pure and powerless, because the power to use it is wanting.

This enduement of the Holy Spirit is the coming of more than nameless power. It is the bringing of the energy of the redeeming personal power of the love of the Lord Jesus Christ. It is the impact of Christ personally by the Spirit. The unity among the disciples is but a small though important part of it. All the Christ is ministered or imparted. And all the gifts and fruits of the Spirit are duly manifested. A lamentable lack of the full symmetry of the perfect sacrifice of the Perfect Saviour through some human hindrance of the ministry of the Holy Spirit does sometimes short-circuit that marvellous current of the Divine Power from heaven.

8. Why has Christianity so-called become so largely an ecclesiastical mausoleum? The rule is not that of the Spirit, and the method not that of the Word; but instead there is a man's wisdom and the substitution of human self-importance exploiting its patent priestly medicine in place of the Redeemer's blood. Another spirit—the earthly ecclesiastical—has in some instances

taken possession of the throne of the Church. Nothing has more demonstrated the patience of God than His withheld judgment and removal of this incomparable hampering and ham-stringing of the Church. Alas, the Church has betimes exchanged the filling from above with that from underneath. Nothing on earth today more needs saving and redeeming than God's own appointed instrument for the evangelization of the world. Alas, alas, the organism of the Spirit has become little more than the organization of selfish human ambition for power over human souls instead of the passion of God to give them the Gospel and Christ, and the Holy Spirit.

9. The baptism or the sealing by the Spirit occurs but once in each individual experience. I Cor. 12:7 says, "But to each one is given the manifestation of the Spirit to profit withal." This suggests that there may be manifestations without profit, which Paul plainly names later on. In the thirteenth verse he goes on also to say: "For in one Spirit were we all baptized into one body, whether Jews or Greeks, whether bond or free; and were all made to drink of one Spirit." This is a deep passage. It is the drinking of the fulness of the Spirit which makes for the constant infilling and the profit of abolishing unspiritual differences and in maintaining the integrity of the body, the church. Invariably there is this profit that the full indwelling of the Spirit secures the fulness of Christ for the member or the church; for apart from the Christ the Holy Spirit never comes at all to anyone or any organization. No filling of the Holy Spirit can dim the reality or lessen

the place and power of Christ over us, for He invariably does the opposite. The more we possess the Spirit of God and are possessed by Him, the more Christ is to us and the more we respond to Him and otherwise appreciate Him. Of His fulness do we all receive in His self-impartation for our personal realization in Him. The ministry of the Spirit always secures by its fulness that our self-realization is in self-fulfilment in the Father's plans and purposes for us.

III. The Holy Spirit's Inhabitation in the Epistle to the Hebrews

1. Beginning with Heb. 2:4, we find, "God also bearing witness with them, both by signs and wonders, and by manifold powers, and by gifts (distributions) of the Holy Spirit, according to His own will." In the preceding verse the writer is warning of the danger in neglecting "so great a salvation," spoken through the Lord, and later confirmed by the Holy Spirit Himself. Here we have the great coöperation and succession of Christ and His work confirmed by the Holy Spirit and His work. It is therefore not a new and different dispensation which we have in the Holy Spirit, but the carrying on to completion that begun in Christ and to which He is as indispensable as at the first. Even so is it in communicating, imparting and perfecting, the Holy Spirit is absolutely indispensable in His presence, wisdom and ministry. What the Lord redeems, the Spirit must inhabit to preserve, develop and perfect.

Here we come again upon the fact that the whole Trinity is inseparably involved in the whole work of

Redemption. The Father plans it all, the Son sacrifices His all for it, and the Holy Spirit gives Himself up to what His Person and ministry can contribute in completing and carrying out all the New Covenant in Christ that He made with the Father for this sorry, sin-bedeviled world. It is so great a salvation by the Son, and the Father Himself contributes everything He has, even the Son Himself; while out of His transcendent resources and fulness, He sends the Holy Spirit in all His immeasurable fulness for indwelling and protecting, and communicating "so great a salvation." Thank God there is back of it the Trinity!

2. In Heb. 3: 7, 8 we read, "Wherefore, even as the Holy Spirit saith, Today if ye shall hear His voice, harden not your hearts."

The Holy Spirit speaks always to the Christian in a very practical way. In every life there are the things that need attention at once. Reading on into this message of the Spirit, we see that He was harking back to the hardening of Israel's heart in the wilderness for forty years. It looks as though all they succeeded in doing was to make an utter failure of a magnificent opportunity. They are the world's model backsliders and heart-hardeners. The old lines of Shakespeare utter the same solemn warning:

> "There is a tide in the affairs of men,
> Which taken at the flood,
> Leads on to fortune;
> Omitted—all the voyage of life
> Is bound in shallows and in miseries."

What is true in the realm of worldly affairs, is also true on a higher parallel in the religious realm. The heart at first grows faint; then hardening from fear, and real cardiac disability sets in. Later on there are bleaching bones on the desert sands. The Holy Spirit called the Israelites to the Promised Land. They had almost reached the land of corn and wine and flowing with milk and honey. They renounced in fear the Divine Leadership. There was no second chance. There could be none.

Today, while it is called today, hear the voice that entreats you to go on to victory and the promised home; and turn not back to the dreary wilderness. When foolish fears are heeded rather than God, faith is failing, has already failed. There is no tomorrow for the soul who today turns a deaf ear and a hardened heart to the leadership of the Holy Spirit, calling, "Forward with Christ!"

3. In 10:15 of this Epistle we have the witness of the Holy Spirit to the New Covenant. "And the Holy Spirit also beareth witness to us; for after He hath said, This is the covenant that I will make with them after those days, saith the Lord; I will put my laws on their heart, and upon their mind also will I write them: Then saith He, And their sins and their iniquities will I remember no more."

The Holy Spirit revealed this New Testament Covenant to Jeremiah. So far as circumstances of the nation were concerned there was no hope other than this. It is so astounding an utterance it is thrice repeated in this Epistle. The Gospel itself could not better state in covenant form these golden words of Divine promise. One thing is certain: the Holy Spirit is not only perfectly in touch with the omniscient, foreknowing Mind of God, He carries the blessed burden of its message forward by controlling in coalescence the prophetic mind of His spokesman.

Here we have the inhabitation of the Holy Spirit in the mind of a chosen man of God who faithfully pens its rich and imperishable promise of a new age, of new relation and new conditions, the New Covenant of Divine Sacrifice and life eternal. What grace was there! What lasting hope! What blotting out of sin! What bestowal of the very utmost that God could impart! That was surely something worth bearing witness to on the part of the Holy Spirit! Shall we not ever remember that God no more remembers our iniquities blotted into oblivion by the blood of Christ?

The New Nature coming by regeneration would naturally be like the Holy Spirit who begets the new born soul with a holy disposition. And the Creator-Saviour in highest order of re-creation in the likeness of His own pure and obedient nature, will crown it all by putting the Holiest Tenant in existence to dwell in that new human heart. That has established the laws of faithful Divine Relation innate and instinctive in human heart and mind. The Holy Spirit is God's most valuable gift to redeemed personality to bring forth growth of power and fruit of service. It is the crowning part of the bequeathment of Christ in the New Covenant, for the Holy Spirit is the power of the law of the Spirit of life working in us in freedom from the law of sin and death.

4. We may look at one more and the last passage from the Epistle to the Hebrews. It is 9:14, "How

much more shall the blood of Christ, who through eternal spirit offered Himself without blemish unto God, cleanse your (our) conscience from dead works to serve the living God?" What is this eternal spirit through which Christ offered Himself? Some take it to be the Holy Spirit. But the Spirit of Christ Himself is as sacrificial as that of the Holy Spirit. And there is the sacrificial Spirit of the Father who gave His only begotten Son for sinners. As already noted, there is no "his" or "the" before "eternal spirit" in the Greek text. What did the Holy Spirit of Inspiration signify by this expression "by eternal spirit"? Surely the one thing left that it can mean is the Spirit of the entire Godhead. This brings us back to the distinctive features of this spirit in each of the Persons of the Trinity. The sacrificial spirit of the Father is sovereign. In the Son the sacrificial spirit is creative. And in the Holy Spirit the sacrificial spirit is fulfilment. The great purpose, task and end of the Holy Spirit is to produce the Holiness of Divine Fellowship in fulfilment. Hence in the appointed Sacrifice of the Son unto the end of the re-creation of the New Covenant, the Son offered Himself without blemish to blot out or annihilate for ever the only thing which stands in the way of fellowship with man and his fulfilment in God. The spirit, then, in this great Sacrifice of Christ in Person was the combination Spirit of the triune Godhead. This is and must ever be Eternal Spirit.

In commenting on the Christology of the Epistle to the Hebrews Mackintosh says: "In the character of Son, also, He offered Himself to God 'through eternal

Spirit.' " This striking phrase almost amounts to a definition of His nature; it denotes that the Spirit which dwelt in Him and made Him what He was, proved to be inextinguishable by death, and thus enabled Him to carry on for ever a priestly work in the higher sanctuary.[28] Then a spiritual death on the Cross was impossible to the Saviour.

[28] The Doctrine of the Person of Christ, p. 84.

Printed in the United States of America

Ingram Content Group UK Ltd.
Milton Keynes UK
UKHW022020070723
424766UK00001B/2

9 781494 051068